The NEW Put Old on Hold

How You Can Stay Youthful Longer and Live the Life You Really Want — Even When Tradition Says You Can't (or Shouldn't)

Barbara Morris

Put Old on Hold Publications

The New Put Old on Hold

© Copyright Barbara Morris 2017

Nothing in these pages should be taken as
medical advice. Information in this book is for
information purposes only and should not be
used to diagnose or treat any illness, disease,
or other medical condition. Always consult with
a qualified medical professional before making
medication, supplement, exercise, or lifestyle
changes or decisions.

Book cover and interior design by Kerrie Lian,
under contract with Karen Saunders & Associates

Published by: Put Old on Hold Publications
P.O. Box 937
Escondido, CA 92033-0937
760-480-2710
author.office@gmail.com

ISBN: 978-0-9667842-6-8

Library of Congress Control Number: 2017937754

Printed in the United States of America

The New Put Old on Hold is dedicated to the memory of my devoted husband Marty, who lived to make me happy. The memory of his love and constant encouragement motivate me to stay strong, growth-oriented and productive... of value not just to myself but to others.

ACKNOWLEDGMENTS

Thanks to author and life coach Joyce Shafer for her contribution, "Six Steps to Create a Vision for Your Life."

Thanks to the amazing team at Karen Saunders & Associates. Karen has expertly brought together a remarkable group of award-winning professionals, including editor Barbara Munson and cover and interior designer Kerrie Lian. I am blessed beyond measure to have had the help and guidance of these talented and dedicated women.

Thanks also to my friend and colleague Mary Lloyd for contributing the Foreword. With gratitude to Dr. Helen Harkness, who brought us together, Mary has a profound understanding of prevailing outdated ideas about aging, which is constant assurance that my revolutionary views are right on.

CONTENTS

FOREWORD

by Mary Lloyd

How you *think* about aging plays a huge role in how you age. Barbara Morris was pioneering a better way to do both long before all the current gurus learned to beat their drums. She looks at the reality of aging with both the eyes of a scientist (she's had a long career as a pharmacist) and the heart of an activist. She was one of the first to champion this worthy fight to make more out of our 50+ years than games of Mexican train and smatterings of exotic travel (or golf and RVing if you prefer that version of the fantasy). Our culture is really screwed up on this whole piece of life. Barbara has been doing her best to find a better way since she was in her 30's. (Five *decades*, folks!)

She hit my radar in 2007, when Helen Harkness (another wise woman about aging) suggested I ask her to write a review of the book I'd just published about finding your own best way to live the last third of your life.

(Supercharged Retirement: Ditch the Rocking Chair, Trash the Remote, and Do What You Love.) When I checked out Barbara's website and newsletter, I was stunned to discover she had a robust body of knowledge and a feisty attitude about "retirement" that was delightfully parallel to my own thinking—but she'd already been sounding the alarm for several years. I dredged up a bit of courage and cold e-mailed her with a request for a review. Bless her, she said yes.

Thus began what has become a deep friendship, in which we have supported and encouraged each other (sometimes through blunt observation) in our professional efforts, but also personally on everything from caregiver burnout to online dating (our current co-adventure). If you want a funny, caring, energizing friend, find someone like Barbara. If you want a much wiser approach to living well after 50 (or so) read her stuff.

I have been asked to write about the updated version of her 2004 book *Put Old on Hold*. I will do that. But it's impossible to address the value of the book without making sure you are aware of the amazing foresight, resilience, and persistence of the author—as well as her unique ability to tell it as she sees it.

The New Put Old on Hold is solid proof that Barbara Morris sees well beyond the stereotypes and time-honored but *wrong* assumptions about "getting older." The truth is coming to the fore with more regularity now, but Barbara's message is still cogent and potent: Most of what we assume is unavoidable and limiting about aging is a *choice*. If we choose to believe—and function—differently, each and every one of us can "Put Old on Hold." Why in the world would we *not* do that?!

It's not a one-time decision though. The "wrong" way is enforced in the media, the entertainment industry, our medical resources, the behavior of friends and family, and our own decisions every single day. "Putting old on hold" is a lifestyle, not an epiphany. It starts with the decision to walk your own road and seek your own best version of a life, but again and again, you will do battle with the lame reality that makes us all invisible and assumes we are ineffective once we acquire some gray hair (or no hair) and wrinkles. That cultural mindset accelerates when we "give up work." Old is perceived as an inevitable affliction rather than a normal and positive part of a good, long life. *The New Put Old on Hold* is full of facts and recommendations on how to ignore all that in creating a life and lifestyle that keeps you vibrant for as long as you live.

The beauty of Barbara's message isn't just in managing to keep ourselves young emotionally and physically though. What she has to say can help us change how the world sees this part of its population. Please read this book and take action. Put old on hold in your own life—for your own sake and for those you love. In doing that for ourselves, we can teach our entire culture a better way to live all the way to the end. The world needs that better way.

Mary Lloyd
Feb 11, 2017

(Mary is author of *Supercharged Retirement: Ditch the Rocking Chair, Trash the Remote, and Do What You Love; Widow Boy* (a novel); and 39 Bites of Wisdom (an e-book collection of articles that originally appeared in Barbara Morris's online newsletter "Put Old on Hold.") She continues to be a resource on nonfinancial retirement issues. For more, see her website www.mining-silver.com.)

THE PURPOSE OF THIS BOOK

The purpose of this book is to "show and tell" older women, particularly those close to retirement, or in early leisure-oriented retirement, that they don't have to experience "old age decline"—a state of being that has nothing to do with physical appearance.

I would like women to understand that wrinkles and sagging body parts are not the cause of or indicative of old-age decline. The culprit is what you allow to go on in your head, and the lifestyle you choose or permit yourself to live.

In spite of the powerful influence of outdated cultural norms and practices, old age decline is entirely possible to overcome, assuming mental faculties are intact. I provide the knowledge and motivation to help you do it. Determination is up to you.

I write from experience. Close to 90, I have avoided age-related decline. You can do it too if you are willing to open your mind, consider some unconventional ideas, and take charge of your life while it's still possible to make decisions that will help you shape your future the way you want it to unfold. The alternative is to do nothing and just allow old age decline to happen to you.

Much of what I write about comes from my experience during my years as a pharmacist. Your knowing that may help explain my position on certain issues and situations.

My intention is to be helpful. I don't expect everyone (or anyone) to agree with me. I make no apologies for my opinions, usually born of insight and experience, and often are contrary to outdated beliefs and consensus thinking. And, because I have a sense of humor, I like to believe I'm always right. (Well, most of the time.)

A "must view" Marc Middleton video (GrowingBolder.com) takes just a little over seven minutes to view and will help get your head in gear to understand and appreciate what's in the pages ahead:

http://tinyurl.com/zxevcfd

IMPORTANT DEFINITIONS

Seniors are traditional. They retire to retire from productivity. They live the traditional leisure-oriented retired lifestyle, and don't want to live any other way. Their credo is "I worked hard all my life and deserve my retirement."

Outliers are individualists who want more out of the older years than what is available in the traditional retirement lifestyle.

Matures are older persons who are growth-oriented and do not see themselves as traditional seniors and don't want to be referred to as "seniors." For the record, I classify myself as both an Outlier and a Mature.

Chapter 1

WHAT I BELIEVE

Traditional leisure-oriented retirement is responsible for more premature decline and deaths than accidents and disease.

No evidence exists that God ever intended that healthy people be put out to pasture in the name of retirement at age 65, or any age.

There is a limit to the amount of do-nothing leisure the mature mind and body can tolerate before turning to mush. Like it or not, we are made for work.

Every healthy retiree living a traditional leisure-oriented lifestyle has untapped potential that will never blossom, grow, and contribute to their community and the world. That potential, along with a lifetime of accumulated wisdom, education, and experience winds up six feet under or burned to ash, stored in a cookie jar and displayed on the fireplace mantle.

I believe you are more powerful and competent that you think you are.

Recognize and celebrate your talents and potential regardless of your age. I believe you can outsmart the ravages of Mother Time and Put Old on Hold far longer than you might imagine. Go for it!

Do you choose to do and be what makes others happy and win their approval, or do you choose to do and be what makes you happy and fulfilled?

–Joyce Shafer, LEC, Author

Chapter 2

RETIREMENT:
An Overview

Today, and in the future, many are not sure they will be able to retire on Social Security alone, given the pittance they will receive upon retirement and assuming, of course, that the nearly bankrupt Social Security system will continue to make payments to retirees.

In his book, *Age Power*, Ken Dychtwald, PhD, says, "Retirement is a relatively new and experimental life that was initially envisioned to last three to five years, not 20 or 30." He cautions that the current retirement model is not realistic for the future.

Of course it's not realistic, but who wants to change it? Even the mere suggestion to raise the retirement age by just one year creates howls of protest.

Possible insolvency of the Social Security system aside, what isn't discussed about retirement is how it affects the body, mind, and soul.

Retirement is a traumatic event with far deeper ramifications than most people realize. It is closure on a lifetime of effort into which you poured your heart and soul. It's a clue the end of life is getting closer. Once the reality of traditional, leisure-oriented retirement is accepted and internalized as a "this is where I am and what I want to be," body and brain chemistry change. Imperceptibly, mental and physical processes slowly shut down. Because the brain is no longer required to perform at a consistent peak level, cognitive abilities begin to atrophy. The cliché, "Use it or lose it" becomes reality.

Consider this: Your last day at work you are somebody—a manager, doctor, lawyer, secretary, or whatever. The next day, your life of

All of a sudden, what you've been (meaning what you've done) most of your adult life has lost its meaning

contribution is over. You are a retired has-been, a person now referred to as "didn't s/he used to be a...?"All of a sudden, what you've been (meaning what you've done) most of your adult life has lost its meaning, not to you or your family, of course, but in the eyes of the world. Your respected status is gone. This loss can devastate self-worth.

Equally tragic is the loss to society of a lifetime of acquired wisdom, skills, experience, and education—a treasure trove of precious assets abruptly abandoned as valueless and discarded in pursuit of a lifestyle dedicated to leisure. Only a culture in decline fails to value the riches stored in the mature brain.

Most financially stable new retirees enter retirement with a brave face, thinking it's going to be okay or—no—it's going to be more than okay...it's going to be fantastic. Free at last! Everything is in place to facilitate the transition: investments, savings and 401K, Social Security benefits, and the traditional naive mindset of new retirees: "I'll have enough money because I won't need as much anymore."

Sadly, even those not financially well prepared for retirement often believe they will be okay in retirement because they bought into the mistaken belief that they will have fewer needs and fewer expenses. A couple of years into retirement, reality sets in—more, not less money is needed.

While it's true not as much will be needed for clothes, transportation, and other work related expenses, inflation has increased the cost of everything: food, housing, energy, health insurance premiums, and especially specialized health care such as naturopathic and chiropractic treatments, or dietary supplements not covered by insurance. Clearly, there was a miscalculation. You need much more than you thought. What do you do if money is running out?

What to do? If you really don't want to go back to work, then pinch pennies, ask for senior discounts, clip coupons, mortgage your home or do a reverse mortgage (financial wizard Suze Orman says don't do a reverse mortgage), economize on food, and take advantage of public assistance programs.

If pinching pennies is not your style, and accepting food stamps or other government programs grates on your self-respect, perhaps you can go back to your old line of work. However, after just six months or a year in retirement, now a lot has changed at your former work place. But the biggest change has been with you. Your thinking has become infected with the "retirement virus" that prefers leisure over effort.

Once your mind and body become accustomed to not having to respond to an alarm clock, and you don't have to get dressed and ready for work when you don't feel like it, you say to yourself when thinking about going back to work, *I just don't want to do it anymore. I can't do it anymore.* You don't want to feel that way, but you do. That's the effect of the resistant "retirement virus" and it's hard to get rid of it.

If you do go back to work for your former employer, you may not like having to learn new routines, deal with new, younger people, or contend with other changes that make you feel like you are starting from the bottom all over again. You keep thinking, *I can't do it anymore. I don't want to do it anymore.* But you need money and, more importantly, you really want to do *something*, because in the deepest recesses of your soul you understand that when growth stops, decline starts. So you settle for less challenging, less demanding, lower-paying work to convince yourself, "I'm doing something of value."

Becoming a greeter at Walmart after you held a prestigious position in your former work life can deal a knockout blow to your self-esteem. You recognize that being a greeter is honest work but it doesn't elevate your status among friends and doesn't make you feel better about yourself.

Not usually taken into consideration at retirement is that the lifespan has increased by thirty years, giving many retirees unexpected 20 to 30 "bonus" years. If money is in short supply in early years of retirement, what will life be like in those bonus years? If you are in financial difficulty, expecting family or friends to step in and take care of you in a manner you would prefer is just not realistic. And "woe be unto you" if you get to a point where you need assisted living or nursing home care. The government will not pay for the kind of quality care you would prefer.

Many people do not spend their work years doing what they really enjoy and chances are you may be one of them. If so, now is the time to take charge of your future.

> *It's critical to manage what goes on in your head and decide what you must do to secure the future you want and not allow life to "just happen."*

If there is a dream job or career that interests you, stop wasting time and start planning to make it happen. Remember, your second life ahead is a blank canvas. Barring a devastating illness or other disaster, you are in control of the kind of picture that gets painted on the canvas. It's critical to manage what goes on in your head and decide what you must do to secure the future you want and not allow life to "just happen."

Assuming health is good, age 50 (if not before) is a good time to start planning for a growth-oriented productive second life. Keep in mind that your age at retirement, whatever it is, is not old! Disregard the ignorance of a backward culture that continues to propagate the myth that age 60 is old, or elderly.

Those who buy into that traditional nonsense handicap themselves, preventing realization of their full potential.

If you still work and are saving for retirement, continue saving even more aggressively, knowing you will use some of that money to help create your new life. Constantly review, improve, and expand your plan. Visualize your future! Visualization is incredibly powerful. In your mind, see yourself successfully doing what you want to do—then visualize this over and over again. Constantly sharpen and refine your vision in great detail. The more clearly you see yourself living your vision, the easier it will be to attain.

Many pre-retirees (boomers) are not prepared financially for retirement. They didn't think or plan ahead and dread the prospect of retirement because they know Social Security will probably not provide enough to live on. Belatedly, they realize there is not a pot of leisure gold waiting for them. Don't let that happen to you. While you still can, plan and save for the future you want. Consider training for a new job or career that potentially would be more rewarding than the one you have now. And, don't ever pay attention to others or the Negative Nellie in your head who suggest you are "too old now" to start a new job or career.

Another reason to save aggressively is that as time goes on you may want to make cosmetic enhancements to your face or body, particularly if you still work and appearance is important, or, you just want to fix things because you want to beat Mother Time at her aging game. In the future, if you have money to do what you want, you will be a lot happier than if you moan and groan when you look in the mirror each day, wishing you could afford to erase some of the wear and tear.

I know you know it but sometimes it helps to be reminded—you only get one shot at life so make things happen while you can because you don't want to get to the end of the road wishing "If only I had done..." If that happens, you will hate yourself and that's not something you want to live with.

I try to practice what I preach. At 86 I got my real estate license, not an easy accomplishment, at least in California. The state exam is difficult and only 50 percent of those taking the exam pass on the first try. The questions are complex, convoluted and loaded with "gotcha" elements, more suitable, I thought, for a law exam than for real estate. I passed on the first attempt. I mention it not to brag (okay, perhaps just a little) but to assure you that if your cognitive abilities are intact, you can accomplish what you put your mind to regardless of age.

Chapter 3

RETIREMENT REALITIES

Not yet retired? Or in early retirement, meaning, in the "honeymoon phase," reveling in your freedom from all the years of work? If you fit either category, there is a lot to think about.

Think about the meaning of the word "retirement." Give it a lot of thought, because it's an extremely powerful word. Ernest Hemingway called it the most depressing word in the English language and I think he was right.

It's important to think about what retirement really means beyond the golf, travel, gardening or whatever retirees are supposed to find fulfillment in doing. When an individual accepts and internalizes the word "retirement," it sets into motion a gradual, nonstop mental and physical meltdown. Your brain chemistry actually changes because your subconscious senses you have chosen to shut

> *When an individual accepts and internalizes the word "retirement," it sets into motion a gradual, nonstop mental and physical meltdown.*

down growth and productivity and, no longer challenged mentally and physically, you are now letting go of life and are preparing for the final event.

While enjoying new freedom in a "living life as a pastime" lifestyle, the decline process happens insidiously, and imperceptibly. Because we are all different, some retirees decline faster or slower than others. Deliriously happy retirees in an active state of decline would be less likely to realize what is happening to their mind and body. A friend may quickly spot signs of deterioration in them, such as slower physical movement, halting speech or changed mental outlook. But most retirees would adamantly insist—and do believe—that nothing has changed, except they're happier than they've ever been.

Here are some retirement realities to keep in mind:

Retirement Reality No. 1:
Loss of Income and Decline in Quality of Life

Financial gurus say you need 70 percent of your pre-retirement income to live well in retirement because unexpected expenses inevitably will pop up and everything seems to cost more and happen more often when you are older. Of course, you can cut back and do without, but where's the fun in that? It would be like starting out in life all over again. Remember how tight money was when you first married and/or began your career? I do! It was challenging to say the least, and penny-pinching lasted a long time.

Who wants to revisit that? After you have worked so many years, your "prime time" is not the time to pinch pennies and clip coupons to pay the grocer and depend on special senior benefits to meet expenses.

To fully understand the significance of needing an adequate income, I wish you could have been in my shoes when I was working as a pharmacist and saw seniors as I saw them every day, relying on Social Security. Sometimes it was heartbreaking. Having $10 to cover the co-pay for medication may not be a big deal when you have enough income, but it's tragic when you don't have it and won't have it until the first of the month when your paltry Social Security check arrives. As if that's not depressing enough, think about seniors existing on Social Security and taking six or more medications each month, with the co-pay for some of those prescriptions costing a good deal more than $10 each. Many seniors on Social Security spend so much money on medication they have little left over for food. Forget about buying vitamins or other diet supplements. That would seem like a luxury to them.

If you want to stay healthy, live reasonably well, and Put Old on Hold, you need money—a lot more than you think, not just for medication but also for quality food and the costly health maintenance that comes with regular use of vitamins, supplements and health care not covered by insurance. I don't care what anybody says, this is not the time of life to even think about cutting back!

Is there a solution? Yes. Many seniors, in spite of health issues, are perfectly capable of working, and they should work as long as it is in keeping with their abilities and preferences. Doing so would keep them in touch with the real world and boost their self worth, not to mention enhance their quality of life. It would be wonderful if government or, better yet, private programs would encourage and prepare healthy retirees, the older the better, to get back to earning a wage. The editor of a senior publication in my area lamented, "Every time I have been told a Senior-Back-to-Work program would be set up, the project falls through...so many qualified seniors are looking for work." Funding is available for so many other social programs, many of questionable worth. Why is it so difficult to get assistance for a program that could radically improve the lives of so many people? Living at the poverty level is the pits when there is an alternative such as having a rewarding job.

Retirement Reality No. 2:
Difficulty Going Back to Work

If you retire for even a brief period, then decide retirement isn't for you, and you try to go back to your former line of work, it may be difficult. I have seen this happen with pharmacists who can't wait to get out of the business. The long hours and stress of dealing with the public eventually take a toll. Then, after six months or a year away from the job, retired pharmacists become bored or need money and decide to go back to work. Unfortunately, the person who retired six months or a year ago is no longer the same person. In that short period of time a person's mental sharpness and physical agility can decline. Speech, movement, reaction time, and the ability to learn have diminished. These individuals are still competent, but their edge is gone. Some pharmacists, recognizing their retirement-induced deficiencies, give up and retreat back into inactivity. It's a great loss of experience, ability and knowledge.

The bridge from the real world to retirement is short, and what's on the other side sounds so alluring, and convenient. If, however, you retire and change your mind and decide to take that road back, you may find it rocky at best or impassable at worst. Of course, if you are lucky, or have made good plans, you may reach a fork in the road that will lead you to a new and exciting place.

Does this mean you should never take a break from work? Not at all. It's important to give your mind, body, and spirit the opportunity to rest and rejuvenate. Periodically you need time away from everything to think, let go of unproductive stress, and allow your brain to process budding ideas and clarify goals. Just be certain you understand the difference between taking a break and "sliding into retirement." When you know you will soon return to something fulfilling, challenging and productive, something you eagerly look forward to tackling, that's "taking a break."

But "sliding into retirement" is deceptively easy. It occurs when you tell yourself you are just taking time to stop and smell the roses. Before you know where time went, no longer do you smell the roses; you are pushing up daisies. Your tombstone reads: "Mary Jones: She stopped too long to smell the roses; she neglected to pursue her dreams and reach her potential. Her would-be greatness is interred here with her remains."

Don't be that woman. Rest (but not too long) and restore yourself, then get on with living, working, and being productive. Fulfill your dreams and develop your innate gifts as long as you live. It's too exciting an adventure to forfeit simply because of chronological age or a misguided social construct called "retirement."

Retirement Reality No. 3:
Loss of Self-Esteem and Personal Power

Many seniors suffer from depression, which can result from a personal loss, major change, repressed anger or painful life event. Those are not the only causes, but retirement, no matter how much you may look forward to it, is a major transition and often a traumatic event. It's closure on a lifetime of contribution. It's saying goodbye to part of you that will never exist again except in memory. It can be no less devastating than the death of a loved one.

One day you have an envied title and an esteemed position in society. The next day you retire and you lose the title and distinction you enjoyed for so many years. Your value has instantly diminished and so has your status. You've gone from being a somebody to a nobody.

How often have you heard it said of someone, "Didn't he used to be a lawyer?" or "Didn't she used to be a surgeon?" I am often asked, "Weren't you a pharmacist at one time?" My answer is, "Yes, not only did I used to be, I still am because I keep my license current by fulfilling continuing education requirements." The reality is, regardless of what a person used to be, like it or not, the expectation of being less valuable or perceived as less competent accompanies the reality of retirement.

Retirement can be particularly difficult for a man who, pre-retirement, held a managerial or other powerful position. One day he is behind a desk giving orders and receiving deferential treatment and respect. The day after he retires, it's all over. A lifetime of establishing identity in his work is gone. And it's gone for good. If he is married, he is now taking orders from a new boss, a wife who likely has been in charge of things on the home front and holds seniority in domestic management decisions. She has her daytime lifestyle and he had his. Suddenly, the man accustomed to being the king of his work castle no longer has a castle or a title. What is he supposed to do now? How do you suppose he feels? How do you think his wife feels? Can you say "major adjustment" that may be difficult and riddled with strife?

No doubt about it: After you retire, your value as a human being and your professional

No doubt about it:
After you retire, your value as a
human being and your professional or
business abilities immediately diminish
in the eyes of the world.

or business abilities immediately diminish in the eyes of the world. You may know in the depths of your soul that you are still the same capable person, but the general negative disregard and feedback don't feed your self-esteem.

How about volunteering? I love it—it's the greatest invention since sliced cheese. It provides opportunity to meet new, inspiring action-oriented people as well as provide new opportunities, especially if you are not yet retired and are looking for new opportunities to get ahead. Once retired, volunteering can do wonders to re-establish a sense of self worth— which I say with some caveats.

I don't encourage volunteer work as a primary retirement activity because, frankly,

I have mixed feelings about seniors working without pay unless they are living above the poverty level. Unfortunately, there is an unspoken understanding that retirees should volunteer because they have nothing better to do.

I have a friend who does volunteer work several days a week. She's only marginally secure financially so I asked why she volunteers instead of having a paying job. She said she would like extra income but because of her age, she doesn't feel qualified to hold a paying job. As a volunteer she feels she works on her terms, which is not entirely true; they wouldn't rely on her as they do if she didn't produce. Because she's been doing the same type of work for years, she's as competent as one could ask. How heartbreaking that she has so little faith in her ability simply because of her age.

Yes indeed, volunteering is noble. It opens the door to a variety of opportunities. It warms the heart and soul to freely help others and expect nothing in return. Such kindness should be encouraged. Yet, there is magic in receiving a paycheck for work well done. It is liberating both financially and emotionally; it boosts self-esteem as little else can, particularly at a time in life when self-sufficiency is not expected or encouraged. I wish it were possible to make a case for paid volunteering. But then, providing payment would negate the meaning of "volunteer." Nevertheless, I think it would be prudent to consider some type of compensation, especially for low-income volunteers.

Retirement Reality No. 4:
Adopting the Senior Lifestyle

In my experience and from what I have seen, many retirees even today live in a narrow, sheltered world in which they see the same people and do the same things every day. They stay close to home, venturing out only to go shopping, to the doctor, or to church. There is little if any challenge to keep their intellect fired up. They sit passively in front of a TV most of the day, unaware or uncaring that the brain and body are turning to mush. They simply find it difficult to keep up with change.

I recall a retired woman on antidepressant medication complaining the world was moving so fast, and she couldn't keep up with everything, particularly computers. It made her feel left behind and this bothered her terribly.

Don't allow yourself to get to such a state. Welcome change, and embrace it. A good way is to stay in touch with young people, who thrive on change. Their outlook and acceptance that change is good will help you see how to Put Old on Hold.

Another aspect of the senior lifestyle is the tendency to adopt a group mentality. Just as teens associate in groups to establish their identity, define their lifestyle, and find emotional support, many seniors become similarly peer dependent. They refer to themselves and their friends as "us old people," "geezers," or "old farts" and take a perverse pride in inviting sympathy, playing up feebleness, describing symptoms and using deprecating terms to describe their age, circumstances, or abilities. They tell each other "old people jokes" that support their decline-oriented thinking and lifestyle. Personal identity, individuality, and independence are lost to group decisions, attitudes, and activities. This observation certainly does not apply to all retirees but I've seen enough of it to view it with concern.

I've also witnessed an irrational group entitlement mentality. For example, at the onset of flu season one year, it became evident flu vaccine was in short supply and scheduled shots were canceled. Most people accepted the situation, but some were irate. One woman called the pharmacy and complained, "But I'm a senior citizen, we're supposed to get those shots before anybody else." Be on guard for unreasonable self-absorption and an entitlement mindset. Whiney, complaining victims forfeit agelessness. Certainly, not all old people exhibit this type of behavior. I encourage you to constantly monitor your mindset and behavior as you age.

Most people living in retirement communities are happy and content. They wouldn't live any place else and that's fine. But I consider it an unnatural segregated environment, locked away and separated from young people, isolated from others who are different than themselves.

Often surrounded by gates, guards, walls, security cameras, with perfectly manicured lawns, topiary, sculptures, waterfalls, and ponds complete with ethereal white swans, retirement communities often seem like a hybrid of a minimum-security prison and a cemetery. It's not an environment that encourages growth and a future-oriented lifestyle. But then, it's not supposed to, is it?

Retirement Reality No. 5:
Unproductive Use of Time

Philosopher and mathematician Bertrand Russell observed the importance of work in his book, *The Conquest of Happiness*[1], in which he states, "Most people, when they are left free to fill their own time according to their own choice, are at a loss to think of anything sufficiently pleasant to be worth doing...To be able to fill leisure time intelligently is the last product of civilization, and at present, very few people have reached this level."

That's a powerful and, yes, a controversial statement. So many seniors in their "leisure time" today prove over and over Russell's observations of the last century.

For example, because so many seniors are in dire financial difficulties, they spend a good deal of time when shopping figuring out how to get the most for their money. While at work, I recall a retiree asking me why something he wanted to buy was $2.00 higher than a competitor. I told him I didn't know and he replied, "Well, why don't you know? It's your job to know." I was at a loss so I gave him an

---

[1] *The Conquest of Happiness*, Reissued, Liveright, Chapter 14, 2013.

800 number to call for a more satisfactory answer. Apparently, the 800 number didn't work out and he was back the next day, asking for a name and address for someone who could answer his question. Perhaps taking on this "problem" and addressing it made him feel productive. Considering how little money Social Security provides, I can appreciate that $2.00 may seem significant.

Here's another example of much ado about nothing when there is little else to think about: My husband and I were living briefly in an enclave of townhouses originally built for occupants 18 and older. There were no walls, gates, or guards; it was just a restricted development in one section of town. Stringent community regulations mandated that pet owners must clean up after their pets. At the time, we had a cockapoodle named Samantha that weighed about 10 pounds dripping wet. Being conscientious pet owners and wanting to be good neighbors, when we walked our little darling we always carried a bag and scooper, wanting to do our part to keep the community in the required pristine condition.

I recall three incidents that gave credence to Bertrand Russell's observation about having too much time to fuss about minor annoyances.

On one occasion, after Samantha left a little pile on someone's lawn, we dutifully picked it up. As we walked away, an elderly man opened a window and yelled, "Stop that! It leaves a terrible smell behind!" What were we to do? We had completely cleaned up the mess. We amused ourselves thinking that on future outings we would carry a can of disinfectant spray and spritz the offending area after picking up. After all, we wanted to be good neighbors.

Another time our little darling took a particularly long time to urinate. When she finally decided she was done and we started to walk away, a woman flung open her door and screamed, "Go back and pick it up!" Well, there was nothing to pick up.

Yet another time, as we were walking past a neighbor, Samantha stopped to leave a few drops. The neighbor, whom we had greeted with a cheery hello glared at us and snarled, "Your dog is staining the grass!" Indeed, some people need something to keep them occupied.

I relate these stories as encouragement to monitor your thinking, behavior, and emotional state closely as the years roll by. Now, while you still have your wits about you, resolve to constantly stay aware of your behavior and mental outlook. As a reality check, evaluate how your social performance stacks up against that of young people. This is not to suggest you emulate their youthful immaturity, but rather, their spontaneity and ability to stay flexible. Your behavior will take care of itself if you continue to remain in the real world, physically, mentally, and emotionally.

Interestingly, I can immediately tell a completely retired senior from one who is still working, even part-time. The person still involved with the realities of life is much more alert, reasonable, and easier to interact with, no matter his/her age. That person is successfully managing the aging process.

If you watch the TV show, "Shark Tank" you may recall seeing a segment that featured a woman who made knitted handbags and employed women in retirement communities to knit some of her handbags. The show featured statements of some of the retired women who explained how happy and fulfilled they felt because they were being productive, creating something of value at their age. It was powerful and inspiring.

The experience of those seniors tells us that if you are in good health, it's smart to

"This is all the growth I want to experience. I'm done."

thumb your nose at tradition that says it's time to retire and not cave in to custom and say, "This is all the growth I want to experience. I'm done." Instead, you will say, "I want to continue to grow and live productively. I will go on, seamlessly, continuing to build, grow and live fully, unconcerned about the number of years I may have left."

Instead of giving in to decline, you will draft your will, purchase a long-term care policy and make other appropriate legal preparations. You will get on with living as if you will live forever. You will ignore the numbers. You will LIVE your life fully and fabulously: ALL OF IT!

Adopt New Stages of Aging

There is another important reason to reconsider a decision to retire. We are living longer—30 years longer—than in the past century. That means you may have many "bonus" years in retirement. Because of that longevity, and because of medical and scientific advances that keep us alive longer, there are new stages of aging we need to think about and how we think about ourselves, relating to worth and competence. If you are able to adjust your thinking and put yourself in a new and different stage of aging, it's liberating beyond measure!

I first became aware of the new stages of aging from my friend and colleague, Dr. Helen Harkness. We are about the same age and she is truly an ageless rock star. I am a slumbering sloth compared to what she has accomplished and continues to accomplish with her super successful career counseling business, Career Design Associates, located in Garland, Texas. In her book *Don't Stop the Career Clock*, on page 79 she reveals her new contemporary model for stages of aging:

> **Young adulthood: 20-40**
> **First midlife: 40-60**
> **Second midlife: 60-80**
> **Young-old: 80-90**
> **Elderly: 90 and above**
> **Old-old: 2-3 years to live**

Isn't that model more realistic than the stereotypical outdated paradigm our culture tenaciously clings to? Doesn't the Harkness model encourage you to re-think where you are in life and, perhaps, help you realize you may have been doing yourself a disservice by seeing yourself as "old" or even "elderly" at the young age you are? Adopt and apply the Harkness chronology that has the potential to change your life!

Having made some negative comments and observations about retirement and retirees, I acknowledge many retired people *are* happy with their lifestyles. They are content and not crotchety; they consider their lives full and even overflowing with activity. There aren't enough hours in the day to do shopping, taking care of the home, cooking, attending classes, gardening, vacationing, golfing, and visiting the doctor. Those blissful people are entitled to do what they want and no one would want to take any of their happiness away from them. They find comfort and satisfaction in the structure and sameness of a day-to-day routine. Indeed, happiness, like beauty, is in the eye and experience of the beholder.

Yet, as I see it, those happy folks are not Putting Old on Hold—that concept is beyond their comprehension or interest. They accept themselves simply as old people and that defines how they live and look at the world. They are going with the flow, doing what they believe they should be doing at their age and they have a good deal of company to prove they are in the right groove.

Having said all of that, I'd add it's important to acknowledge the two good reasons to start unplanned traditional retirement:

1. You simply don't want to work anymore.

You are tired of taking orders from a boss half as smart as you are. You want to be your own boss and finally do what you want and go where you want when you want. After all, you've worked long and hard and you've earned your retirement. You are understandably tired. Social custom says it's time. You are ready for the senior lifestyle. Your friends are retired. You want to travel. You want to live how they live. You'd like to crank up the RV and get on the road with your significant other. Or maybe, you could even take a trip around the world. You are ready to play Bingo, enjoy early-bird discount dinners, hang out at the senior center, and play cards or shuffleboard with like-minded peers. Maybe you'd go back to school, and maybe take classes and learn to use a computer. In short, you want your liberation from the daily grind and the conformity of a daily job.

2. You retire because you don't have a choice.

There are lots of reasons to retire. Your health may have given out and you are unable to continue to work. You may need to take care of ailing parents, or one or more of your children or grandchildren. Your spouse may require your full attention. Or your employer may find a way to prematurely replace you. Yes, there are legitimate reasons to retire, and under more favorable circumstances you might have made a different choice.

Let's look next at the value of actively pursuing lifelong growth and productivity.

Chapter 4

MATURE PRODUCTIVITY VERSUS TRADITION

According to Discovery channel "Dirty Jobs" star, Mike Rowe, "Work is a beautiful thing." It is, indeed, regardless of age.

Retirement is not part of the Ten Commandments and I am not aware of any edict handed down by God that retirees must move to the Saucy Seniors Retirement Village at some specific age.

My mother, who worked to support herself until age 92 when she passed away, was really good at identifying the true nature of things. Sharp as a tack, she never considered retiring and if you had asked what she thought about retirement, she probably would have called it an "invention of the devil." Mom was rarely wrong, which I learned many times, often later in life.

But, look, who wants to work until the day they die? You probably recoil in horror at the thought, but some Matures do plan to die with their boots on, and I'm one of them. I am joined by increasing numbers of savvy pre-retirees who intend to be productive after retirement because they want to; they recognize what productivity can do to make life satisfying, exciting, and more fun than they had when they were younger. If they remain healthy they will be among the lucky ones who will have a truly enviable, fulfilling second life, even with hitting speed bumps and potholes along the way.

That said, it's important for working adults at any age to strike a balance between work and leisure. Unfortunately, for older people, sometimes it can be difficult to strike that balance. Fueled by subtle reminders from friends and the culture that "life is short," eventually leisure wins and decline settles in.

Let me be clear: I'm not advocating an end to traditional retirement. That would be a monumental waste of time and effort. If you want to live the traditional retirement lifestyle, you should have that option. But I am calling for choice. There also should be another culturally sanctioned alternative lifestyle for the retirement years that encourages and legitimizes balanced productivity as a respected, even preferred lifestyle.

What do I mean by "balanced productivity"? It's simple. It means that before you retire you have a post-retirement lifestyle plan that includes ongoing growth and productivity interspersed with "work breaks" that allow you to enjoy the fruits of your labors. All work and no play makes no sense. It is important to be sensible about when you "work or play" and how much time you allot to each.

If living a productive lifestyle in the retirement years gains traction and becomes a status symbol, would those who want to live a traditional retired lifestyle feel guilty or less respected? Is it possible that traditional retirees might be negatively judged the same way traditional young moms sometimes feel judged when they choose to stay home and raise their kids instead of going to work? Would there be some conflict? Probably, and that's not a bad thing.

I believe that eventually there would be a coming together of the best parts of both cultures. If fully accepted by the culture as a respected alternative to the traditional decline-oriented lifestyle, the result would be a healthier more independent older population—a tremendous health, financial, and social benefit.

There will always be those who say, "Be happy where you are in life. Don't listen to masochists and workaholics who encourage you to work if you don't want to. Traditional retirement is time to enjoy yourself." If you are in agreement with that idea, then honor what you feel and believe. Just be ready to accept the mental and physical decline that accompanies deliberate, unchallenging inactivity. If you decide to just let life happen, you may find yourself in your "bonus years" in a nursing home, looking back and wishing you had done things differently. Or, maybe not. Just understand the likely consequences of following tradition and giving in to your human nature that prefers leisure over effort.

Old Age Decline and the Business of Retirement

The word retirement means what it says: you stop doing what you have done most of your adult life, and when the event takes place, life abruptly changes forever. Yesterday you had a job and you were a somebody; today you are a retired nobody—you are over the hill. Even though you may have been looking forward to the day you hang it all up, it's traumatic. Your mind and body are in a tailspin. You feel neither "here nor there." What happens next?

Lacking a plan for an alternative retirement lifestyle, you will become part of the traditional senior lifestyle—a way of life and mindset that has grown and evolved gradually since establishment of Social Security. It is a lifestyle dedicated to leisure and unfortunately the mind and body are not designed to flourish with mind-numbing non-stop leisure. As a result of a longer lifespan, 20 to 30 years of "retirement leisure" is a guarantee of huge numbers of old people in varying stages of premature decline with all the accompanying social, health, and financial issues.

Unfortunately, our culture doesn't address the calamity resulting from "retirement leisure" because retirement *per se* is not recognized as a cause of, or even a contributing factor in "old age decline."

For a couple of reasons, retirement itself is not acknowledged as contributing to decline. The main reason is that it is part of our culture—an entitlement. Any argument, however eloquent, that leisure-oriented retirement is not ideal for healthy older people is usually drowned out by "We worked all our lives and deserve our retirement." Perhaps when Social Security is finally out of money we will agree to rethink the retirement phenomenon, which was not expected to last more than two or three years for most people, rather than the current twenty or thirty.

Another reason traditional retirement is not viewed as contributing to decline is the prevalent belief that "old age decline" is unavoidable regardless of how we live because that's just how life works. We are not supposed to live forever. Those who appear to outsmart Mother Time—those who seem eternally ageless—are anomalies. Maybe so, but we are witnessing more and more so-called ageless anomalies who are proving wrong the belief that "old age decline" is inevitable. These ageless wonders have found the secret that unlocks healthy longevity—but it's *not* a secret. It's just not recognized or accepted by a culture that prefers and supports tradition over progress when it comes to understanding and dealing with aging.

Moreover, traditional retirement is not acknowledged as contributing to decline because it is Very Big Business. Consider the amount of money spent on so many facets of the retirement experience. Products and programs of every kind dealing with housing, travel, personal care, medical services, and everything between are targeted to retirees at every income level. Clearly, the retirement industry is lucrative and it's here to stay because it satisfies the needs and wants of retirees and caters to, and services, retirement decline. This is not to say there is anything wrong with businesses that serve the retirement culture—you just have to wonder why so many of those businesses not only exist, but thrive.

If more healthy Matures continued in the workplace or in their own businesses rather than retiring, their standard of living and quality of life could improve significantly. Their needs and wants would be different than their younger cohorts, creating opportunity for development of different types of businesses to serve them. Would the traditional retirement industry be adversely affected? Not likely. Businesses that provide value adjust and survive.

So, what's the difference between businesses that serve traditional retirees and those that cater to productive retirees? It's simple. One services the needs resulting from a leisure-and-decline oriented lifestyle while the other supports the needs and wants of those living a robust, contributing, productive lifestyle. Think about the significance of that difference and what that difference says about the vibrancy and health of the culture.

Now, on to retirement communities.

Chapter 5

RETIREMENT COMMUNITIES— THINK HARD BEFORE YOU MOVE IN

I suspect there will be more disagreement with my take on retirement communities than with anything else I write about in this book. No, I don't think retirement communities are a good idea. I suppose I shouldn't say that because many retirees love their communities and are happy living in them. Nevertheless, I consider them unnatural living environments segregated by age and often by income.

By their structure they support an insular mindset and lifestyle that can encourage an entitlement-tainted "us against them" attitude in relation to the outside world. For example, years ago when swine flu was a threat, vaccine was in short supply and given first to those considered most vulnerable. As mentioned earlier, at the pharmacy I got a call from a senior, distraught that those in her community were not first in line to receive available shots. I assured her everything was being done to take care of those most in need of the vaccine, but she persisted with her "us against them" tirade, convinced advanced age entitled seniors to preferential treatment. Perhaps they are entitled to be served first; it was the entitlement attitude that was irritating.

At retirement age, if you worked most of your adult life, even at a job you liked, chances are you are really, really tired, mentally and physically and you are eager for the new and exciting life of leisure you conjured up in your imagination. You don't think about a possible downside about what you have been looking forward to so eagerly because in your mind there is no downside. You are giddy with expectation, anticipating the pot of "leisure gold" at the end of the work rainbow. You don't realize that rushing to get to the Saucy Seniors Retirement Village with blinders on your eyes and without a plan to be productive may portend an old fogey, rusty, rigid retirement.

In their youth, boomers declared they would never get old and they believed it. They are now starting to retire, still believing they are young, looking for fun, still smoking pot (some or many still do), and where are they finding a good time? In activity-oriented retirement communities.

Many retiring boomers who declared the certainty of their eternal youth now gravitate to the same retirement havens as their parents. For example, upscale retirement communities in Florida, already populated with older retirees, pitch their appeal to the live-for-today boomers in much the same way Disneyland is marketed to fun-loving kids and their parents, offering an array of enticing freebies and social activities available seven days a week—golf for life, tennis, Jimmy Buffet (or other boomer icon) concerts, dances, parties, book clubs, trips to museums or wineries, travel to exotic places, or classes on everything from basket weaving to the intricacies of existential thought. What's not to like?

Realistically, it's essentially regimented living-life-as-a-pastime stuff—nothing much that creates the kind of positive challenge that keeps the brain fine-tuned. It's fun without a doubt, but the resulting unanticipated decline can be costly.

New boomer residents of established retirement communities seem unconcerned that lots of old people are already there, frolicking (with their leaky bladders) in the community pool, playing shuffleboard, bingo, or enjoying other passive activities that appeal to traditional retirees. But that's okay. Boomer retirees don't have to take part in traditional activities with the older crowd. They can hang out with the margarita-swilling sexy swingers and swap venereal diseases they never knew existed until they moved to the Saucy Seniors Retirement Village.[2] They can enjoy all the boomer attractions, reliving the time they were feral and free teens, in a paradise surrounded by youthful peers still believing they will never get old. Here's the thing: as time goes on and new waves of retirees arrive, established boomer retirees become part of the shuffleboard crowd—and they never saw it coming or thought they would see the day they would become one with the old folks.

[2] http://www.nytimes.com/2014/01/19/opinion/sunday/emanuel-sex-and-the-single-senior.html?_r=0

Imagine, living in a walled cloister of sorts, populated by old clones of yourself trying desperately to keep alive the belief "we will never get old" in Margaritaville.

Imagine, living in a walled cloister of sorts, populated by old clones of yourself trying desperately to keep alive the belief "we will never get old" in Margaritaville.

Unfortunately (or fortunately—depending how you look at it) in an active retirement community, after a couple of years of doing "young" things with "young-minded" people, one day you may wake up and realize the retirement honeymoon is over. The OMG! moment has arrived. You are at a party and all of a sudden reality hits. You think, OMG! look at all these boring old people and you ask yourself, *What am I doing here—what am I doing with my life?*

The OMG! moment generally happens if in your former life you really enjoyed being productive and you had a particularly satisfying job or career. In retirement you have become restless, perhaps outliving your money; you start reminiscing about life as it used to be when you had a purpose and plenty of money, and when what you did really mattered. You realize how much your thinking has slowed and remember how sharp you used to be. You bring to mind satisfying moments of your work life as you cook for the routine potluck community dinner, where after-dessert gossip passes for entertainment. You miss the stimulation and interaction with supportive co-workers and friends. Yes, your work was stressful much of the time, but this retirement lifestyle is often stressful too.

As time goes on, if you become less active because of health issues, or you no longer drive, and perhaps have fewer connections and contacts with the outside world, fellow residents, as boring as they may be, become an important part of your life. You don't like to rely on them for companionship and support, but you feel stuck with them. You are annoyed with them constantly griping about neighbors, gossiping about meaningless community stuff and/or complaining about aches and pains. You resent the negativity. You begin to think you would rather be surrounded by a mix of healthy, lively people again who inspire productivity and growth. But now you are resigned that you are where you are.

Eventually you will deal with a depressing and concentrated amount of sickness and death—more than if you were living in the larger world. Life starts to feel like a soap opera or depressing TV reality show, featuring disenchanted, bored and boring "The Real Retirees of Saucy Seniors Retirement Village."

So, again, asking yourself, "What am I doing with my life?" after just a couple of years in traditional retirement probably means you are not a typical traditional retiree but a closet Outlier. (More about Outliers in Chapter 9.) You would like to be productive again. While some friends and family may support your thoughts of exiting from the golden ghetto, other voices will discourage you with, "At your age, why bother?" or "You are too old now" or "Let it go—life is too short, enjoy it."

The "you are too old" rebuke is cruel. To a mature woman, little is more depressing or discouraging than hearing "you are too old" to do what you want to do and know you can do. I don't care how old you are; if you are in relatively good health, you can acquire new skills that will get you back into the outside world, doing something growth-oriented, useful, and of value, not just for you but for others. Easier said than done? Perhaps; but if you want something enough, you will dig deep for your latent strength and potential and bring it to life.

It's not your imagination—you know your mind and body are slowly turning to mush and you want to stop the decline. If nothing else, perhaps it's time to become an Avon lady or sell Tupperware. Real estate for an older person is a great gig that can produce excellent income. As I mentioned earlier, at 86 I got my real estate license and am affiliated with a company that specializes in selling luxury homes. Using your mind and body to create a more interesting productive life beats drowning in boredom and depression and dealing with decline.

If you are retired and feel you are done with mind-numbing "fun and games," there is still time to plot your exit strategy back into the real world, to do your part to change cultural norms that are stuck in the past. Please read Joyce Shafer's guide later on in this book, "Six Steps to Create a Vision for Your

Life" to help you turn your vision into reality. Just keep in mind that your "back to the real world" plan must embrace a significantly different mindset and lifestyle. Freedom awaits!

Now let's move on to the "secret sauce" that affects how well you do or do not age.

Chapter 6

IT'S ALL ABOUT YOUR HEALTH

When you are in your retirement years nothing will determine the quality of your life, your happiness, and the happiness of those around you more than the vitality of your health.

Having and maintaining good health is more important than money, sex, power, or relationships. With great health, having enough money is not a worry (you can still earn), sex is better, power is awesome, material things are a pleasure, and relationships are what you choose to make them.

Optimum mental and physical health in the older years provide liberation beyond measure. It is so freeing that it boggles the imagination. Excellent physical and mental health will enable you to revel in life over age 70 and beyond. I guarantee it.

Please don't assume that, as you age, decline is inevitable. While it's true that as time goes on, in spite of best efforts to have the best health possible, you will likely have unforeseen problems, some minor and irritating, and others, much more challenging, such as dementia or cancer. In spite of the unforeseen, if you try diligently, as early in life as possible, to safeguard and improve your health, growing into old age fairly uneventfully is entirely possible. Prevention pays off.

When you get to a healthy age 60, you can look forward to a rich second life, free to do what you've always wanted to do. The youthful struggles of "getting there" will be gone. You will "be there" and you can use your valuable past life experience to grow on. Your second life can epitomize the essence of Martin Luther King Jr.'s proclamation, "Free at Last! Free at Last!"

In relatively good health, you can go back to school, begin a new career, start a new business, start a new relationship, or whatever. You can have a job that provides a great standard of living rather than just getting by on Social Security. If you are in good health and have adequate income, you can enjoy some of the finer things in life rather than having to spend your money on medication, and inexpensive, low nutrition foods.

When you are healthy and strong, you don't have to worry about being a victim of mental, physical, or financial abuse, or fall prey to social systems that limit your freedom or security. The best part of staying healthy may be the freedom you give to your children. When you are 60, 70, and beyond, and in great health, your children, with inevitable problems of their own, won't have to worry, "Will we have to put Mom and Dad in a nursing home?" or "Will they have to (God forbid!) live with us?" or "Will we have to help them pay their medical expenses?"

The benefits of good health are too great to pass up. Make the effort for yourself, your kids, for society. We all benefit from each other's good health.

Your Health: It's Your Personal Responsibility

One hard truth we have to accept is that traditionally trained doctors don't know as much as they should or could know about how to stay healthy. In medical school and during residency, training primarily consists of learning how to use diagnosis, intervention, and medications to treat illnesses and to save lives. Little consideration is given to nutrition and prevention, the most basic aspects of maintaining health[3]. Although this is slowly changing because traditionally trained doctors are beginning to see the light and are educating themselves about the value of nutrition, it's not happening fast enough. That means you should take care of yourself. That means you should educate yourself about the role poor nutrition can play in a health problem, as well as how improved nutrition can change the course of an illness.

If you have a health problem, you owe it to yourself to learn as much as possible about the impact of diet and nutrition on your condition so you can become an informed participant in your treatment. Please understand I'm not suggesting you tell your doctor what to do. Think "partnership." The key is informed participation. Research, information and knowledge will empower you to make intelligent choices about the treatments your doctor may suggest...or suggest some yourself.

I have often been told by patients that they disagree with their doctor's evaluation

---

[3] http://ajcn.nutrition.org/content/83/4/941S.full

or treatment of their condition, but they go along with it because "the doctor said so." I personally feel it's insane to hand your body over to someone, however highly credentialed, and say, "Here's my body. Do with it what you will." Please bear in mind you don't have to obediently accept every treatment your doctor recommends. Never forget: It's your life, your health, and it's your body, so take responsibility for it.

If your doctor resists your informed participation, find a physician who will listen to you. Your doctor is not God, but if that's the way you see him or her, find another medical deity. Some are better listeners and more open minded than others are. Some will even pray with you if that's your inclination.

If you are healthy and don't have a significant health problem, now's the time to make certain one doesn't develop, if at all possible. I don't subscribe to the theory that just because your parents had cancer or diabetes it will be your fate. Perhaps your parents didn't live a particularly healthy lifestyle, even though they thought they were doing all the right things. Perhaps they didn't drink or smoke, but most likely they ate the disastrous all-American diet, unaware of the role it played in the condition of their health.

I'm convinced that paying attention to lifestyle choices can break the chain of many seemingly inherited diseases such as diabetes, high blood pressure, heart disease, and even cancer. You have far more control than you may think.

Love and value yourself. Your mind and body are all you will ever have, and they must last a long time. When you value who you are and what you have, you are less likely to abuse yourself with the wrong kind of food (or too much of it), alcohol, tobacco, and destructive lifestyle choices.

Your health is not your spouse's responsibility, your parent's responsibility, your children's responsibility, the government's responsibility, or your doctor's responsibility. Your health maintenance is your responsibility. If you don't know where or how to start to take charge of your health, here are a couple of suggestions.

Find the right help

Many traditionally trained doctors are becoming integrative physicians, learning about nutrition on their own via credentialed courses that should have been taught in medical school. How do you find one of those doctors? For starters, check out the American College for Advancement of Medicine at ACAM.org. One of my favorite books that offers comprehensive information and wonderful resources is *10 Reasons You Feel Old and Get Fat* by Frank Lipman, MD.

Find a naturopath well informed about nutrition. He or she is a health professional who will likely know good books and other resources for you to read and study. My current favorite book I just mentioned above and I'd mention other favorites here, but they change quickly as soon as I find other books I like even more! A good place to learn about nutrition and new nutrition books is on public TV stations, which often have shows featuring prevention-oriented professionals. Copies of show presentations can usually be purchased through the station's online store. It is on one of those shows that I became aware of Dr. Daniel Amen, who specializes in brain health.

One of my favorite magazines is *Life Extension* (Lef.org). Current issues of the magazine are available on the site and I highly recommend that you check it out. I also read Dr. Julian Whitaker's "Health and Healing" print newsletter, which I have subscribed to for years. His site, Whitakerwellness.com provides great information. He is one of those rare traditionally trained medical doctors oriented toward achieving and maintaining good health as naturally as possible.

I like naturopaths because they diagnose the state of your health and nutrition needs primarily on the basis of comprehensive blood tests two or three times a year. Such tests reveal many things including cholesterol levels, hormone levels, assorted nutrient needs, and even genetic predispositions. Relatively inexpensive blood tests of all kinds are available through Life Extension and are usually listed in the Life Extension magazine. Along with the Life Extension tests, free consultation with a Wellness Specialist is offered to help interpret results.

A comprehensive test helps detect potential problems before they gain a toehold. Even though the Food and Drug Administration (FDA) mandates regular blood testing if you are taking certain medications, traditionally trained doctors usually do not order comprehensive blood tests.

Perhaps the most important reason to have a comprehensive blood analysis is to check on how well your liver and kidneys are doing, particularly if you continually take prescription medication. Adverse reactions to prescription medication contribute to the death of some 200,000 people per year. That shouldn't happen. If tested often, drug-induced liver and kidney damage could be uncovered before it results in disability or death.

With a comprehensive blood test a naturopath can advise you on which supplements to take that will meet your personal nutritional needs. Many people on what I call a self-directed "health kick" will go to the drug store or health food store and buy a bottle of vitamins advertised on TV—or they purchase whatever supplements a sales person recommends. This is all too common and it is a hit or miss approach to wellness that may be better than nothing, but may also be a waste of money if what you buy is not what you need.

The downside of working with naturopaths, if it can be called a downside, is that they often do not accept insurance plans, and that's unfortunate. I have health insurance but because I get most of my health care needs through a naturopath, I pay out of pocket for most of the services I need or want.

My recommendation to establish a relationship with a naturopath does not mean you don't need, or shouldn't have, a relationship with a traditional primary care physician. There are times when you will need that relationship also, especially to be admitted to a hospital, or if you need tests that a naturopath does not provide, or medication or services that naturopaths do not offer or prescribe. In other words, keep all your options open. Just understand the limitations and benefits of each type of health care provider.

No Butts about It

It's hard to believe, but many people still smoke. If you smoke, decide you are going to quit—then do it.

At one time (back in the dark ages!) it was cool and sophisticated to smoke. You were encouraged to smoke and cajoled into starting, one way or another, with misleading health and safety claims, or relentless advertising that influenced you to put that first cigarette between your lips. But remember, you made a choice. Even after the first puff made you sick as a dog, you chose to persist.

Regardless of why you began, adopt a defiant attitude and refuse to see yourself as a victim or having a "disease." Be a victor, not a victim. You can do it. This is where your primary care physician can help with a prescription for a smoking cessation medication. Be aware these medications can have very serious potential side effects, but they can help you quit.

As you improve your diet and get on a regular exercise program, you will most likely find your craving for tobacco diminishes.

Here are some well-known facts about the dangers of smoking. If you smoke and are on the fence about giving it up, this may spur you to action:

- *Each smoked cigarette burns away eight minutes of your life.*

- *Smoking a pack a day translates to losing a month of life each year. Smoke two packs a day and you can sacrifice 12 to 16 years if you are a lifetime smoker.*

- *Smoking compromises the immune system so severely that it takes at least three months to reverse the damage to your immune system once you quit.*

- *Smoking one pack a day depletes 500 mg. of vitamin C, more than most people absorb in one day.*

- *Cigarettes elevate the carbon monoxide level in the blood, which so ruthlessly competes with oxygen that it takes the circulatory system six hours to return to normal after just one cigarette.*

I hope this information helps motivate you to stop. Smoking truly sucks. It sucks the life out of you.

Smile!

The older you get, the more significant a nice smile becomes. It can take years off of your appearance and influence how others interact with you. While nasty looking teeth may be a social turn-off and age your appearance, what's more important is the health of your gums. My dentist tells me that 50 percent of his midlife patients have some degree of infected gums. That means bacteria from a low-grade infection constantly circulate though the body causing vague aches, pains, and other symptoms that seem to have no apparent cause. The bottom line is this: if you are not seeing your dentist regularly, you are doing your health and possibly your social life a grave disservice. Who wants to kiss someone with yellow, brown or missing teeth?

If your teeth are crooked and it bothers you, don't hesitate to get braces (yes, even at your age—especially at your age!)...either the traditional "train track" variety or Invisaligns. I first had traditional braces on my teeth at age 60, later moved on to Invisaligns and I loved them. I still wear retainers at night. If your teeth are yellowed with age, ask your

If you are not seeing your dentist regularly, you are doing your health and possibly your social life a grave disservice.

dentist about bleaching them, or, if the budget allows, consider veneers. It will take years off your appearance.

Taking care of my teeth is one of the smartest things I have done to improve my health, appearance and help me Put Old on Hold.

Next... health care realities.

Chapter 7

HEALTH CARE REALITIES

The public is growing disenchanted with health maintenance organizations (HMOs) or any kind of third party insurance. Members of HMOs see consumer costs rising and the quality of health care declining. It's not your imagination that co-pays and policy premiums have reached the level of obscene, and if you think things are bad now, get ready for what is on the way unless some drastic changes are made.

Expensive drugs will continue to appear on the market and be advertised directly to consumers, creating a demand for them. This method of advertising is called "Direct to Consumer" advertising, or DTC. It is extremely expensive and adds astronomically to the cost of prescription medications. DTC drives ailing consumers to the doctor's office demanding a prescription for the latest magic bullet. The doctor complies with a prescription for the advertised medication, presumably first having read information (particularly about side effects and potential interactions with other medications) supplied by the drug manufacturer. The patient, feeling victorious about having a prescription in hand for the most advanced medication, has visions of an instant relief or cure and hurries to the pharmacy to claim the treasure. Then reality sets in. The patient's HMO doesn't want to pay for the new drug, protesting that older, less expensive medications work as well.

If the doctor really wants the patient to try the new medication, she may have to spend time convincing the HMO why the patient needs the expensive remedy. If the HMO refuses, as it often does, and the patient really wants the new drug, the patient pays full price out of pocket. Then the distraught patient wails, "Why does this medication cost so much?" Part of the reason is the expensive and effective DTC advertising that drove the patient scurrying to the doctor's office to ask for it.

Should you be in a hurry to try an expensive new medication that may have disturbing side effects? Are you willing to risk a bad reaction to gain a doubtful benefit? Are you fully informed about the consequences of your decision? It's often difficult to make an informed decision because of the way drugs are advertised.

How carefully do you pay attention to side effects rattled off during TV commercials for prescription drugs? You should; it's an education. For example, one advertisement says medication designed to alleviate arthritis may cause sudden, unexpected internal bleeding, or liver or kidney damage. (Remember, such drugs are considered "safe" and okay to market to consumers by the FDA. Is that crazy, or what?)

Another advertised medication declares it may possibly cause flu or ear infections. Is that possible? How can medicine cause flu or an ear infection? A virus causes flu, and bacteria cause infection. Another widely advertised new medication to control diabetes has a genital yeast infection for both men and women as a possible side effect. If you do some research about the medication you will learn that the "genital yeast infection" as it applies to men refers to a foul smelling discharge from the penis, pain, rash, redness, itching or swelling of the penis. It is considered a less common side effect but if a man is in a relationship, and experiences that side effect, he may have difficulty explaining away the nasty "genital yeast infection" that looks and feels like something a lot worse.

The commercials are so cleverly crafted that what remains in the viewer's mind is not the litany of possible horrendous side effects but the powerful visuals, depicting happiness and that catchy music that suggests the promise of relief. Those commercials sell an enormous amount of medication. If they didn't, the pharmaceutical companies would not spend tons of money on TV ad campaigns.

To be fair, when talking about the high cost of prescription drugs, other cost factors come into play. For example, U.S. pharmaceutical companies give away billions of dollars in free samples each year, an amount that increases every year. Samples are given to doctors, who give them to low-income or indigent patients. Sometimes they are given to patients to get them started on a medication.

In addition to drug sampling programs, some drug companies have direct patient assistance programs that provide no cost or low cost supplies for low-income or indigent patients.

It's one thing to be aware of the sampling program and another to see it in practice. Recently, while in my traditional doctor's office waiting for my appointment, several drug manufacturers' sales reps came in with huge bags filled with medication samples. It reminded me of kids at Halloween with their trick-or-treat bags. Those free samples represented a lot of money.

Another reason for the high cost of medication is the astronomical amount of money poured into research and development of many promising drugs, which often turn out not to work as expected and are abandoned. When a new drug is effective in clinical trials, it must then go through a lengthy and extremely expensive process of approval (or rejection) by the federal Food and Drug Administration (FDA) before marketing can proceed. This too, adds to the high cost of prescription drugs.

The best option for you is to take care of your health so you don't have to take a ride on the medication merry-go-round. Maybe you won't avoid it entirely, but you can—more often than you might think possible. Freedom from having to take medication is a priceless prize to pursue.

Health Care Rationing

Health care rationing is closing in and the older you get the more momentous this issue becomes. Rationing means if you need or want a particular medication or a surgical procedure, whether or not you get it may depend on a committee that weighs the pros and cons of necessity in your situation. Be prepared—your age may be factored in to a negative decision.

I recall an article in 2001, "Rationing scarce life-sustaining resources on the basis of age."[4]

It concluded: "In certain circumstances, rationing by age is both morally permissible and justified. However, the capacity to benefit from treatment has to be considered whatever the age of the individual and any measure of benefit needs to take a broad range of medical, ethical and economic factors into account."

Does that seem reassuring to you? Not if you are over seventy!

I believe that with appropriate lifestyle choices and nutritional enhancements, it's possible to considerably reduce the need for expensive medical care. Obviously, you can't eliminate all health problems from your life.

[4] J Adv Nurs. 2001 Sep;35(5):799-804

Certainly, bad things happen to good people who do all the right things. But with intelligent lifestyle choices it's possible to substantially reduce the odds of bad things happening and significantly improve your ability to have an exceptional quality of life far longer than you thought possible.

Free Yourself From Fear of the Future

There are two major reasons people fear declining health in the older years. The first is what is experienced and observed through the course of life, and the second is social conditioning. You see people whose health is declining, so it seems inevitable it will happen to you eventually. Purveyors of gloom and doom give credence to your assumptions and observations.

How often do we hear that a certain amount of short-term memory loss is normal, starting as early as the mid-forties? It can become a self-fulfilling prophecy, giving permission to let down your guard, inviting decline by thinking "I must be getting old" when memory lapses occur. Everyone experiences memory lapses. They are like momentary traffic jams that clear up as quickly as they start. Don't believe something bad will happen just because "they" say it will.

Through the years I have worked with many conscientious, bright young people. Typically, they attend school and are involved in sports. Some have two jobs. And guess what? When there's a ball game or an exciting event coming up, they sometimes forget what they are supposed to do on the job. They apologize, but never once has any one of them attributed a memory lapse to their youth. And why should they? Young people focus on youthful concerns while older people worry about what older people worry about.

Do not accept the possibility of memory loss without a plan of preventive action. Consistently, persistently, and intelligently work to improve your memory and do what is necessary to hold on to your mental competence. I help myself by subscribing to online brain games including Lumosity and BrainHq by Posit Science. I buy memory game books such as *399 games, puzzles & trivia challenges specifically designed to keep your brain young* by Nancy Linde with a foreword by my favorite brain doctor, Dr. Daniel Amen. Watch for his

very informative shows on your public television station. I take supplements to support
mental acuity. For fun I do crossword puzzles
and build websites.

When memory lapses happen, let them
be, without fearing you are losing it, or tell
yourself you are getting old. Stay strong in
your belief that you can remember whatever
you want. Until and unless a qualified expert
diagnoses Alzheimer's or other form of dementia, believe that your memory is working well.

Fear of decline accosts you in so many
ways. I've seen an ad on TV in which a boomer-
aged woman says she isn't afraid of growing
old, but she is worried she won't be able to
afford the cost of medication. The unspoken
message says you will need medication as
you age and that decline and deterioration
are inevitable. That is the worst kind of fear
mongering.

It would be wonderful if public service
announcements assured people that if they
would take responsibility for achieving optimum health, they wouldn't need to worry so
much about the cost of health care. Remember, great health is not the result of visits to
the doctor or taking medication. You achieve

great health by what you choose to do for yourself, day by day, year in and year out. Lifestyle choices matter.

The Gorging Epidemic

It's easy to understand why so many Americans are overweight. Fast food is everywhere; restaurants of every imaginable variety, and supermarkets with delis are just a few minutes away from home or office. There is continuous and relentless exposure to availability and advertising of ingestibles of all kinds, fueling the desire to try this or that tasty product.

On many talk and news shows, cooking segments are the norm. Reality cooking game shows create celebrity chefs who promote themselves, their kitchen gadgets and their skills on home shopping shows. Eat! Eat! and Eat some more! Obesity, anyone?

The reality is, we have been trained to eat, even when we're not hungry. We eat for emotional comfort, for social approval, to defuse anger, relieve boredom, or depression. We eat because "it's there."

Food abuse is eating calorie-dense, nutritionally bankrupt "stuff" over a long period of time. You know the culprits: fried anything, refined sugar, and processed junk foods. And don't forget pickled, preserved, freshly embalmed or processed meats contaminated with bacteria.

According to U.S. Department of Agriculture scientists, in 2000 Americans ate 140 more pounds of food than in 1990. Do you think we are eating less today? Or how about this: The average American eats 152 pounds of sugar each year. According to Coca Cola's own figures, the average teen consumes 65 gallons of its product each year.

Americans now spend more than half their food budget on food outside the home. The lust for unhealthy food is not abating. It's unfair to blame the prevailing obesity epidemic on heredity. We have become a nation of food gorgers and abusers.

If you are a self-proclaimed "foodie," resolve to get over your love affair with food. Stop watching TV food shows. When food shopping, don't buy stuff you know you shouldn't eat. If it's not in the house, you can't eat it. Do not swap stories with friends or coworkers about a great new restaurant you discovered that serves mega portions, or how much you stuffed yourself at dinner last night. "Food talk" supports, condones, and encourages over-consumption.

When you see a TV or print advertisement for food, look at it objectively—don't allow the enticing visuals to override your intelligence. Think critically and decide how you are going to react. Constantly remind yourself how much you value your body and your life and that you will not abuse it with food.

When you try to tame the gorging, the desire for food may become an irrational, possessive lover. When you take an "I don't love you anymore" attitude about overeating, food becomes a stalker, constantly tempting you to eat, whispering, "Try this, just one little bite won't matter." Recognize the temptation for what it is and deal with it firmly.

Now that I've excoriated the all-American preoccupation with gorging, how about fasting? A concept as old as the Bible, fasting, particularly intermittent fasting, is now gaining acceptance among some medical practitioners. There are degrees and types of fasting and should be done with the help of an integrative physician or naturopath.

Fasting doesn't mean having to starve. One or two days a week you can fast on juices as well as water to keep you up and running. Fast on a day you don't go to work or do anything too strenuous. If you have a juicer, you can have an enjoyable, beneficial fast using a variety of fresh fruits and vegetables. But fasting is not for everyone. If you are diabetic or have other health problems, check with your physician first.

Some of our cultural eating habits are as out of date as many of our ideas about aging. For example, why do we eat three meals a day? It may have been appropriate in another era when more people performed hard physical labor during the day, but today, are three hefty meals really necessary, or would eating smaller meals be more desirable? Let's face it, we tend to eat too much too often. I often think we are "eating ourselves sick."

Some of our cultural eating habits are as out of date as many of our ideas about aging.

Stamp Out Food Abuse

Look, you can't treat your body—your temple—with disdain and disrespect for the first 50 years, stuffing into it the worst elements of the all-American diet, and expect your body to run like a trouble-free Mercedes for the next 50 years.

You can change your diet if you really want to. You weren't born loving greasy burgers and fries, buffalo wings, fried mozzarella sticks, deep fried Twinkies and Snickers bars. Once you make a commitment to your health and make the lifestyle changes that will enable you to Put Old on Hold, you will eagerly want to eat what's good for you. You will treat your body with respect. You will learn the magic and joy of eating to live instead of living to eat.

Along the way on your resolve to change your way of eating you will suffer relapses, and that's okay as long as you stay focused and don't use the lapses as an excuse to give up. It's okay to have an occasional dessert, or glass of wine. It's okay to have breakfast at McDonald's once in a while. The key word is occasional.

Food abuse is encouraged in TV commercials. Don't believe ads that suggest you can eat mountains of indigestible stuff masquerading as food and then pacify the resultant stomach upset by popping a pill or drinking an antacid. That is wrong-headed. Your body can tolerate food abuse for just so long before you develop serious problems. You will eventually experience chronic intestinal distress. Your liver will begin acting up. Your cholesterol will pile up. Your arteries will start to clog. Your gall bladder will rebel. If not that, you make yourself vulnerable to a host of other disorders. We've all seen overweight comedian "Larry the Cable Guy" in commercials for Prilosec that suggest it's okay to eat greasy food and defuse the ensuing "heartburn" with a pill. That angers me. "There ought to be a law!"

Seductive food ads would be meaningless without a place to buy what is advertised. Take a look at the layout of your favorite market and in particular, scrutinize the mile-long aisle of shelves loaded with breakfast cereals. Just about every home in America starts the day with puffed, popped, flaked, or shredded faux food fortified with vitamins because processing destroys the nutrients originally provided by Mother Nature. What makes them appealing are taste, texture, lots of sugar and scientifically developed flavorings that make you crave more. Then there is the influence of unquestioned tradition. "We always had Rice Krispies for breakfast when I was growing up." Is that your story?

When my daughter was little, after watching a TV commercial for corn flakes, she asked me to buy a box. She was relentless and I finally gave in. Guess what? In her innocent, innate wisdom, she "yukked" at the soggy, sloppy mess in her bowl and never again asked for corn flakes or any other pseudo cereal product.

People leave for a day of work after eating a bowl of sugary cereal then are hungry for real food a few hours later. Their blood sugar, having spiked after the surge of sugar in the cereal, has plummeted. They are now craving donuts and coffee for an energy pickup.

At the same time, kids are sent off to school loaded with enough sugar from breakfast cereal or toaster pastries to send a rocket into space. When they can't sit still or concentrate, behavioral specialists are called in and may decide the sugar-shocked kids have Attention Deficit Disorder (ADD). The cure is a narcotic drug that turns kids into obedient, submissive zombies. Certainly, nutritional deficiency is not the only reason youngsters exhibit ADD or ADD-like behavior, but it's a significant reason.

Judging by the number of prescriptions filled for Ritalin, Adderall, and similar drugs prescribed to control ADD, one would think there was an epidemic of maladjusted or brain-damaged children. Before prescribing drugs, wouldn't it make sense to examine and improve the diet? If that doesn't work, at least it would get kids started on a course of sensible food choices.

When I was a child, ADD was unknown. I don't recall classrooms in chaos with kids unable to behave or concentrate. Children sat in their seats and learned what the teacher taught. The few students who decided to demonstrate "attention deficit" behavior cooled their heels in the principal's office until the misbehavior disappeared. At that time, sugary, lifeless breakfast cereals were not a staple in every home. During the depression years, breakfast was a cheese spread (protein) on whole wheat bread (not processed white fluff erroneously called bread). Or maybe even eggs, if the budget allowed. From a nutrition standpoint, it was a lot better than what most children from poor and affluent homes alike now eat every morning.

Although the nutritional content of breakfast cereals has improved in recent years, don't kid yourself—much of it is still pseudo food. It has little more nutritional value than shredded or flaked cardboard or puffed Styrofoam, regardless of what advertising says about vitamin fortification.

If you want to eat bran type cereals, at least read the labels carefully and decide if the high carbohydrate, low protein, or high fat and minimal vitamin content of the products is worth the price. When you read labels, you will surely conclude that for your breakfast perhaps you can do better with nutritious, whole grain bread (which still has its vitamin and mineral content) slathered with cottage cheese, almond butter and a drizzle of honey.

You might consider eating oatmeal, which almost cooks faster than you can pop a pastry into the toaster, and you will then have something nutritious at a fraction of the cost. For a fast dose of protein, how about eggs? I know they aren't recommended if you have high cholesterol, and experts warn us not to eat more than a couple a week. Should you follow that advice? It all depends on which experts you listen to. I am convinced eggs are not deserving of the bad press they have received. They are an excellent source of protein, and if you are cutting carbs, you couldn't ask for much better. I love eggs and eat them every day, and my bad cholesterol is low. Eggs don't have to be boring—there are dozens of ways to prepare them.

Constant overload of sugar really abuses the body. Chronic sugar-laden coffee and caffeinated soda junkies (this includes diet soda as well) and donut dunkers can forget about Putting Old on Hold. They will go through blood sugar surges and slumps all day and this takes a toll. They don't realize it but they are begging to be the diabetics of tomorrow.

Take into consideration that it's our free enterprise system at work enticing you into making food choices. The purpose of creating an ingestible or processed food product (or any product, for that matter) is to make a profit. That's okay; profit makes our economy work. The variety of products available allows you to make choices. Simply be aware and think when deciding what you will put into your mouth.

Regardless of your age or state of health, I bet I can predict what you are thinking: "Give up what I love to eat for a benefit I may not realize until far into the future? You have to be kidding! Give up my two-martini business lunches, nutritionally bankrupt breakfast cereal, greasy whatever, hot dogs, chips or cheese dips? Give it all up for salads and veggie burgers? No way. I feel great. There's nothing wrong with my health. I'm going to be just fine." Sorry, you won't be fine. You will likely be sick and old just when you could be starting a healthy, vigorous second life.

The body is incredibly forgiving and often responds miraculously to intelligent, aggressive, loving care. If you are now aware that you've fallen prey to food abuse, or poor food choices, you can help compensate by taking supplements, chosen after a comprehensive blood analysis and consultation with a nutrition-oriented medical doctor, naturopath or integrative physician.

Yes, taking supplements is important. If or when you ask a traditionally trained physician if you should take a vitamin supplement, chances are the doctor will say, "If you eat a well-balanced diet, you don't need vitamin supplements. You are throwing your money away." That's what he has been taught. It doesn't mean his advice is correct.

I would like to ask doctors who say "we get everything we need in our diet" to explain their definition of a well-balanced diet. They probably live on the same deficient all-American diet as most of their patients. As already mentioned, medical school gives short shrift to nutrition and wellness education. This is slowly changing but we have a long way to go. Since the American Medical Association (AMA) recently changed its long-standing opposition to vitamin supplements and now recommends at least one multi-vitamin a day, some doctors may change their attitude. But I wouldn't count on it happening *en masse* any time soon.

On a website for pharmacists, I read an article titled "Is Too Much of a Multivitamin a Bad Thing?" The premise of the article was that everyone gets enough vitamin C and other nutrients in the diet. Not taken into consideration by the author, I guess, is the vast amount of nutrient deficient fast- and processed foods that are the main diet of many children and adults.

The article began:

"Healthy individuals can easily get enough vitamin C through diet alone. In fact, based on a 2,000-calorie diet for healthy adults, half of one 2.5-oz package of Kellogg's Fruity Snacks provides 100% daily value (DV) of vitamin C. If you ate the entire package, it would provide 200% DV."[5] I thought to myself, here is another ignorant attack on supplements by a supposedly informed person in the medical profession. The author of the article is a doctoral candidate.

I decided to Google the ingredients in Kellogg's Fruity Snacks and learned the following:

Ingredients: CORN SYRUP, SUGAR, APPLE PUREE CONCENTRATE, WATER, MODIFIED CORN STARCH, GELATIN, CONTAINS 2% OR LESS OF CITRIC ACID, MALIC ACID, VITAMIN C (ASCORBIC ACID), NATURAL AND ARTIFICIAL FLAVORS, RED 40, BLUE 1.[6]

Since product ingredients are labeled starting with the largest amount to the smallest amount, from that description, it is

[5] http://tinyurl.com/zbu39co

[6] https://www.kelloggs.com/en_US/.../kellogg-fruity-snacks-sours-product.htmlKellogg's

clear the product is mostly sugar, and at the bottom of the list, some vitamin C and other ingredients including food dyes "Red 40 and Blue 1." Food dyes are known to be egregious health offenders so I Googled those two dyes[7] and this is what I learned:

- *Blue #1 (E133) and Blue #2 (E132): Banned in Norway, Finland, and France, studies have shown them to cause brain cancer and inhibit nerve-cell development. The colors are found in candy, cereal, soda drinks, sports drinks, and pet food.*

- *Red #3 (E127) and Red #40 (E129): While Red #3 was banned [in the U.S.] in 1990 for topical use, it can still be sold on the market in our foods and beverages. Red #40 may contain the carcinogenic con-taminant p-Cresidine and is thought to cause tumors of the immune system. In the UK, it is not recommended for chil-dren, and it is currently banned in many European nations. The dyes are found in fruit cocktails, maraschino cherries, gren-adine, cherry pie mix, ice cream, candy, bakery products, and more.*

---

[7] http://www.rd.com/health/conditions/rainbow-risks-6-artificial-food-colors-you-need-to-know-about

It is tragic that medical students are not provided with reputable information that provides different facts and references than what they are currently given in medical school. Unfortunately, education in medical *and* pharmacy schools focuses on diagnosis, and the use of drugs to mitigate symptoms of a diagnosis.

As an aside, the pharmaceutical drug industry could not flourish without medical and pharmacy schools teaching students about drugs created by the pharmaceutical industry and how they are needed to treat various illnesses. Once out of school and in professional practice, those students become the main avenue of distribution for drug industry products they learned about in school and, yet, no one questions that arrangement. Before drug companies co-opted the profession of pharmacy to train pharmacy students to use the industry's products, pharmacy students were taught to use and prescribe mostly natural substances, found in nature. Granted, pharmaceutical companies have created many useful drugs we wouldn't want to be without, but in doing so, it also destroyed pharmacy as a truly legitimate and needed profession.

No wonder students graduating from these schools know next to nothing about the role nutrition plays in achieving or maintaining wellness. No wonder students blindly discredit and sneer at information that doesn't support what they have been taught. The result is that the public health suffers.

You don't have to suffer professional bias or ignorance. Read labels, and if you can't pronounce ingredients, that doesn't necessarily mean they are bad. Dig for facts until you get a clear understanding of what you should or should not ingest if you care about your health. It's not that difficult.

By the way, the principle that I try to follow, when looking for answers, be it politics, nutrition, or most anything else, is Herbert Spencer's admonition:

> "There is a principle
> which is proof against all information,
> which is proof against all arguments,
> which cannot fail to keep man in
> everlasting ignorance;
> that principle is—
> Contempt prior to investigation."

You have the ability to think and reason. Use that ability to make your health better. Be determined. Set-in-concrete thinking takes time to change.

If there is one thing medical practitioners fear, it's the scorn of their peers. They consult with each other about what's acceptable practice. A mainstream doctor doesn't want to be considered a kook by colleagues. Being perceived as a supporter of alternative therapies often puts a doctor in a questionable category if his thinking is considered too radical. A good example is what happened to Nobel Prize winner Linus Pauling. He was a respected and celebrated scientist and anti-war activist until he made known his controversial views on the benefits of high dose vitamin C. After that, his status as a credible scientist diminished in the medical community. Although his research on vitamin C is now more accepted among some in the medical profession, he never regained his once revered position among many of his peers.

Medication Mischief

Supplements are often critical for those taking prescription medications. For example, oral contraceptives deplete the body of vitamin B-6, folic acid, vitamin B-12, vitamin C, and the minerals zinc and magnesium. What is the significance of these depletions? For one thing, depletion of vitamin B-6 reduces synthesis of serotonin, which can result in depression and anxiety. Could that explain why many women on oral contraceptives also take antidepressants? Depletion of vitamin B-6 also reduces synthesis of melatonin, which can cause sleep difficulties, and raises homocysteine levels, which can damage arteries, increase plaque formation, and boost the risk of cardiovascular disease.

Diuretics or water pills can deplete potassium. So-called "loop diuretics" such as furosemide (Lasix) can deplete calcium and magnesium. Calcium loss is significant for older women at risk of osteoporosis, especially in their later years.

A substance called coenzyme Q10 (usually referred to as CoQ10) protects the heart and is vital for cellular energy production. It is so important for those taking a statin drug, which can often cause muscle pain and weakness, but how many people taking a statin drug know enough or are encouraged to supplement their diet with CoQ10 (available without a prescription)? Cardiovascular drugs can cause CoQ1O depletion. Potential depletion problems manifest as congestive heart failure, high blood pressure, and generalized low energy. Unfortunately, we don't always get the whole picture. This is another example of why we need to take responsibility for our health.

An aside about statins: I recall a male mid-life patient on a high-dose statin complaining about muscle pain and in particular, memory issues. He related how he had called his mother, and having forgotten that he called her, called again the following day. He said these issues surfaced soon after starting on a statin. He discussed his concerns with his doctor, who did nothing more than switch the patient to a lower dose statin, which didn't seem to help. The patient continued to complain about the same issues.

From my perspective, there are two types of medication: (1) Those needed for conditions such as seizures, infections or some medical condition that can't be controlled or managed except with medication, and (2) medications taken to control or alleviate symptoms caused by poor diet and lifestyle choices.

Unnecessary use of medication to remedy lifestyle-induced problems results, in part, from the prevailing thought that it's okay to abuse your body with food because you can fix it by swallowing a pill. I have already mentioned it but it bears notice again—the TV commercial featuring comedian "Larry the Cable Guy," who suggests to viewers that Prilosec can relieve their "heartburn" and then he triumphantly holds up a greasy chicken leg. Recent news questioning the safety of Prilosec-type medications called Proton Pump Inhibitors (PPIs) are unsettling to say the least. Among many reports coming to light about their dangers, the February 2017 issue of *Life Extension Magazine* has a well-documented article exposing the "Hidden Dangers of Heartburn Drugs."

Problems with Multiple Medications

Many patients experience severe or disturbing side effects while taking multiple medications. This is what can happen: You take medication "A" for arthritis. While alleviating some pain, it causes stomach and intestinal upset. So your doctor prescribes medication

"B" to offset side effects of medication "A." In turn, medication "B" has side effects of its own. It may cause drowsiness or nausea. You tell the doctor about these side effects and he prescribes medication "C" to control the drowsiness or nausea. In turn, medication C may create other problems such as itching. Before you know it, you may be taking four or more medications. And you wonder why you don't feel well. This is especially a problem with older people.

Yes, medication is also necessary to control diabetes and run-away blood pressure. Medication helps lower nasty cholesterol and other problems that plague our self-indulgent culture, but diet and lifestyle changes may help just as much.

Yes, medication is necessary to control pain, infection, seizures, and even some conditions you were born with or acquired. There are many legitimate uses for medication and we would suffer needlessly without the relief they provide. However, most medications, when taken over an extended period of time, are extremely hard on vital organs such as the liver and kidneys. Prolonged medication use, necessary or not, will seriously impair your ability to

Put Old on Hold. Your goal should be to acquire optimum health so you won't need to rely on medications to get you through each day.

What I've mentioned here is just the tip of the iceberg. Continue to keep yourself informed. Understand what medications not only can do for you, but to you.

Be in the Know

Here's some insider medication information you might not find elsewhere. I hope this will really get you thinking. In a pharmacy there are different categories of medications. Here are just a few:

Antibiotics

Cholesterol control

Contraceptives

Gastric disorder relief

Pain relief

Mood alteration

Blood pressure regulation

Hormone replacement

Respiratory relief

On the list above, only one category of medication can produce a cure: antibiotics.

The rest only alleviate or manage symptoms. Think about that. Could diet and lifestyle have a bearing, to some degree, on conditions represented in the categories above? Absolutely.

In a supermarket pharmacy, customers come to the prescription counter with shopping carts overflowing with the makings of their all-American diet: manufactured, synthetic, pseudo food, loaded with grease, refined sugar, salt, assorted chemicals. Even processed, so-called "fresh" meat that may be in an advanced state of putrefaction and bulging with diarrhea-inducing bacteria. Then customers pick up prescriptions for high blood pressure, high cholesterol, gastric upset or arthritis pain. With better diet and lifestyle choices, I believe they might need far less medication.

Older people trapped in the cycle of food abuse and prescription drug relief may be living longer with the help of their medications, but often they are not living well. I can't count how often I heard the complaint, "I'm taking all of the medication my doctor prescribed, and I still don't feel good." These were old people in every sense of the word. They can't Put Old on Hold. The only thing that's on hold is a visit from the Grim Reaper.

They can't Put Old on Hold. The only thing that's on hold is a visit from the Grim Reaper.

Here is something I read in a pharmacist's magazine that made me angry:

"As members of the baby boom generation approach their senior years the retailer is preparing to handle the record number of prescriptions they will certainly require."[8]

Will you "certainly require" a record amount of prescription medication as you age? No, you should not, if you start taking care of your health right now. The same article stated: "The aging boomers want to remain young and healthier longer, and this will translate into prescription drug therapy to accomplish these goals." Prescription drug therapy to help stay younger and healthier longer? I think not. Remember, with the exception of antibiotics,

---

[8] "Retailer ready for aging boomers": Chain Drug Review, December 16, 2002 p. 28

most drug therapy just relieves or manages symptoms and does not cure health problems or promote good health.

Start to take care of your health early on and keep it up because clearly, vibrant health does not come out of a prescription bottle. It results from how well you care for yourself over time. It's a test of how much you appreciate and value the one and only body you will ever have.

Some History About Drugs

Today's drugs are like nothing in the past. When I was a child, my father's drug store was a naturalist's delight. Bottles and packages of pharmaceutical grade roots, leaves, stems, bark, flowers, and berries lined the shelves. Pharmacy as a profession was called "The ancient and noble art of the apothecary"—now a dinosaur, thanks to the pharmaceutical drug industry that co-opted it for its own financial gain and destroyed *pharmacy* as a profession. Those natural ingredients were used to make tinctures, syrups, elixirs, and concoctions of every description to treat everything from sore throat to syphilis. I remember a sore throat remedy my father made and sold as

"Iron Mixture." It was the most vile-tasting stuff you could possibly imagine, but it quickly relieved a sore throat. Were some of those botanicals harmful? Potentially, but doctors and pharmacists knew how and when and in what form to use them safely.

Then, as now, nervousness was a common complaint (we call it stress today) and Elixir of Phenobarbital was the drug of choice to soothe the symptoms. It was so popular with doctors and patients that my father dispensed gallons of it in a very short period of time. Also then as now, stomach and intestinal complaints were common, but a mixture compounded of three or four herbal ingredients made life bearable.

Health insurance as we know it today did not exist. People paid out of pocket for what they needed. A prescription might have cost a customer 50 cents or $1.00 for a month's supply and patients got a refill whenever they asked for it. Government had not yet interfered in our lives as it does today, telling us (or controlling) what we can or cannot take when we want it.

It wasn't until the appearance of penicillin, followed by more powerful antibiotics, that medication usage began to change. For example, before penicillin, when kids got a cold, it was allowed to run its course with the help of simple remedies to alleviate aches and fever. After penicillin, It didn't take long for doctors to start prescribing penicillin to avoid possible "secondary infections" when a child had a cold.

Yesterday's drugs (before penicillin) were relatively benign compared to today's highly complex, laboratory-engineered substances targeted for specific ailments and often producing an exhaustive list of strange or dangerous side effects. For example, a medication called cimetidine (Tagamet), used to treat stomach problems, is also said to eliminate plantar warts on the bottom of the feet. Think about that. A medication created to target a specific area of the body (stomach) can affect another area of the body in a very unexpected way. Are there other sleeper side effects of other drugs, formerly requiring a prescription, now sold over the counter and available to anyone?

Here is the bottom line: Open your mind. Learn as much as you can about medications you may be taking. Your health is your responsibility so take care of it as best you can.

Water, Water Everywhere, But Who Drinks It?

Do you drink an adequate amount of water every day? What is adequate? A friend carries around a pint bottle of water and sips it occasionally. She is convinced she drinks enough water. No, it's not nearly enough!

I believe many problems traditionally associated with old age are not the result of the aging process, but the result of dehydration. When I counseled customers about their medication, I routinely asked how much water they drank. Many people said they don't like water, that it made them nauseous, bloated or that it made them urinate too often.

I vividly recall an older woman complaining that her saliva was thick and she had sores in her mouth. I asked how much water she drank and, predictably, she said, "I don't drink water. It makes me sick to my stomach." No amount of scolding would have encouraged her to drink more water. Sadly, she was drying up from the inside out. This woman was mummifying herself. A word of caution: If you are not a water drinker, and you start to drink large amounts of water all at once, it's reasonable to expect you may feel nauseous because you are stirring up stored toxins.

What kind of water is best? I have a filter system under the kitchen sink that takes everything out of the water. I know I'm doing the right thing when I see the condition of the filter when it is changed once a year. The gunk on it from municipal water is disgusting.

While some water contaminants result from natural sources such as pathogens from wildlife and toxic minerals that leach from ground minerals, I am concerned about sewage, industrial waste, pesticide runoff, illegal dumping, unused medications, and just plain defective and/or inconsistent treatment. I don't think purification systems in any municipality are effective enough or completely trustworthy.

No amount of scolding would have encouraged her to drink more water. Sadly, she was drying up from the inside out. This woman was mummifying herself.

I can grudgingly accept chlorine in the water because it's used for purification. However, chlorine reacts with naturally occurring organic matter, resulting in the formation of trihalomethanes (THMs), known to cause rectal and bladder cancers and birth defects. As for fluoride, I know all the arguments in favor of adding it to the water, but it is not a benign substance. A major use for fluoride is to kill roaches and ants. While minuscule amounts may be good for preventing cavities in teeth of children or preventing osteoporosis in older people, I don't think it's wise to mass-medicate entire communities. It negates personal choice.

Exposure to fluoride occurs in toothpaste, mouthwash, chewing gum, children's vitamins often given from birth, and other sources of which you are probably unaware. How much is too much? How can you know how much fluoride you are ingesting when it comes from so many different sources? I don't know of any study that proves fluoride does not accumulate in the body. I often wonder if exposure to excessive fluoride plays a role in the development of Alzheimer's or other common degenerative diseases.

As I've already mentioned, I have an under-counter filter system that removes everything from water. What about gadgets you attach to your faucet? Or counter top pitcher-type filters? Pitcher filters improve the taste but probably don't get rid of fluoride, pesticides, bacteria, and poisons such as lead, mercury, or arsenic. Lead-based paints are no longer used but drinking water may still be fed through lead pipes. It is estimated that over half of the cities in the United States have lead or lead-lined pipes in municipal systems.

As for bottled water, anything labeled "purified" or "drinking water" is just tap water cleaned up. You take a chance no matter what brand you buy.

Cold water is a natural appetite suppressant. Try it when you feel hungry, particularly if you ate just a short time before.

Hunger pangs are often a manifestation of hidden thirst. A woman asked me about the effectiveness of weight loss products because nothing she tried had worked. When she said she was always hungry, I asked how much water she drank. "Hardly any. It's overrated," she snapped. When I told her hunger was often a sign of hidden thirst, she grinned, narrowed her eyes, and smirked, "Yeah, right." Some people want to hear only what they want to hear.

Learning what it takes to Put Old on Hold is not difficult if you are disciplined and willing to learn strategies that work and are willing to put them into practice. It also takes an open mind and the ability to consider information that may be contrary to what you believe as the "gospel truth." Before moving on, please give this Herbert Spencer admonition (which I gave earlier) your serious consideration. It works for me and can work for you:

> "There is a principle
> which is proof against all information,
> which is proof against all arguments,
> which cannot fail to keep man in
> everlasting ignorance;
> that principle is—
> Contempt prior to investigation."

Now let's move on for my personal take on "staying young."

Chapter 8

"HOW DO YOU STAY SO YOUNG?"

I am often asked: "How do you stay so young?" Right now I'm 88.

I have learned "how to stay young" but for some reason, when I'm asked for my "secret" I don't seem able to explain it in a way that younger women understand. The usual response to my explanation is a smile and a condescending, "That's interesting" or, "That's great" or, "You must have good genes." My explanation is simple: In order to "stay young," it's imperative to avoid the traditional senior mindset and lifestyle. Yes, other things are involved, but "staying young" is what I just said it is: *Avoid the traditional senior mindset and lifestyle.* If you think you are old, if you think you are too old to continue to learn and grow, if you live a traditional retired lifestyle—it's all going to have a significant impact on

If you think you are old, if you think you are too old to continue to learn and grow, if you live a traditional retired lifestyle—it's all going to have a significant impact on the condition of your body.

the condition of your body. **The body follows the brain! Your body becomes a reflection of what you think about and how you live.** Obviously, it takes some additional explanation, but basically, that's it.

I really do understand why many younger women don't "get" my explanation. If you are in your thirties or forties, your head is in a different place than it is when you are in, or close to, retirement. At a young age you are not ready to hear or understand my explanation because for you, retirement is the least of your concerns; it's not even remotely on your radar. In other words, in order to understand my explanation you have to be at or near retirement age. You have to be thinking about

128

it and what it might involve. You have to be open to listening to ideas that are not conventional. Of course, if you are a perceptive young person and you "get" my explanation, that would be extraordinary. That would put you far, far ahead in the aging game. You are destined to be youthfully ageless, provided that at your retirement, you remember what I told you when you were years younger.

Let's Start Here

At age 76, working as a pharmacist in a supermarket pharmacy, I decided to turn in my starched white jacket and regulation corporate tie. I did not stop working to retire, I just needed to be available for a family member and I wanted to focus on writing. There was a lot I wanted to say to encourage older women to make the effort to Put Old on Hold.

My decision also gave me more time to work with computers, which I enjoy in a perverse sort of way. Dealing with a computer is often a frustrating experience, which is okay because I thrive on aggravation. If you can survive working in retail pharmacy dealing with cranky customers, struggling with computer code is a piece of cake. I now use my writing and techie skills to build websites and publish the monthly online *Put Old on Hold Journal*. I encourage you to subscribe:

www.PutOldonHoldJournal.com

You are also invited to visit my personal website at *www.BarbaraMorris.com*

I have written several books to help boomer women avoid the pitfalls of aging. They are listed at the back, under Resources. (So much for tooting my own horn.)

What I Learned While "Doin' Drugs"

The pharmacy I worked in served a large middle income senior population. It gave me a bird's-eye view of an ordinary senior lifestyle and traditional retirement, and what I heard, saw, and was told in confidence was pretty disheartening at times. People tell their pharmacist everything and I listened intently because I knew what I was hearing was providing a priceless education. Listening to accounts of retiree traumas and triumphs made clear to me what I had to do and not do in my own life as time went on.

I often said to myself, as I listened to an unhappy retiree, "There, but for the grace of

God, go I." I realize that sounds insensitive and unkind, but to me, traditional retirement was a depressing way to live the final years. Even retiree fun activities seemed boring and an affront to their intelligence, but when you don't have anything better to do, and not much money, you do anything to kill time. Favorite retiree pastimes included spending mornings or afternoons hanging out at the local coffee shop reminiscing about the past, playing bingo or shuffleboard at the senior center, or gambling at a casino with money they could ill afford to lose. I recall one woman who objected to having even a small co-pay for her prescriptions because she said she needed money to gamble.

Casino buses would stop at designated places around town and pick up seniors. That bothered me for a couple of reasons. First, as I've already mentioned, many seniors did not have enough money to gamble, and they would skimp on food and/or medicine to have money to feed the slot machines. The other reason is that I felt the casinos would be doing a far better thing for seniors if they took them to classes or other venues for enjoyable activities that would actually improve the quality of their lives. I realize that's a pie-in-the-sky expectation but it would have been a terrific public relations opportunity.

The feistier widowed women made up their faces and dressed to the nines as they chased each other's boyfriends (in short supply), not for sex (they insisted) but for companionship. One lothario in particular was a favorite—tall and slender dapper Disco Danny, who wore polyester suits and ostentatious jewelry from the 1960s and smelled better than any of the ladies. He had a full head of tight curly white hair that he attempted to fashion into an afro. To complete the look he wore funky tinted eyeglasses reminiscent of those worn by John Lennon. He certainly was an eye-catching dude. The women loved him, not just because his "coolness" took them back to a happier time, but he also could drive and run errands for them.

The married men followed their wives around like panting puppies; when they got the chance to interact with a younger woman, their remaining testosterone flared up and they got a bit grabby—not in an offensive way but grabby nonetheless. When I was out of the pharmacy area and on the selling floor helping a customer with a product, I was the recipient of an eager arm around my shoulder more than I liked but I understood the "why" of it. Without question, the men and women alike suffered from touch deprivation, a condition common to lonely retirees. Someone to hold them close once in a while would have alleviated some of their need to feel wanted and connected with other human beings, and perhaps even help mitigate some of their health issues. I used to think that at least some of the multiple medications taken by seniors could be replaced by a warm hug and some kind words every day.

Women much younger than I am would say, "Barbara, don't ever get old. It's the pits." They weren't just despondent about health issues, they were dealing with boredom and running out of money, and as I've just mentioned, money they had often wasn't spent wisely. Jack Daniels was a daily companion for many of them—an abusive and expensive relationship, frequently preferred over food. The amount of wine and whiskey in shopping carts was shocking. It was particularly upsetting to me because I knew how much medication they were taking that should not be taken with alcohol. Their prescription containers had warnings about alcohol, but who reads those tiny warning labels? I made more than a few verbal warnings that went in one ear and out the other.

A few had part-time jobs, but for the most part, in spite of financial problems, they would not consider any type of employment. A common comment was, "I've worked hard all my life and I deserve my retirement." One time I made the mistake of asking a coupon-clipping retired (younger than I) engineer if he had considered part-time work. I asked because in addition to his fondness for coupons, he always complained about having a small co-pay for his prescriptions. I realized immediately I should not have asked that question because he snappishly assured me he had earned his retirement and would never consider working again.

Those proud "I earned my retirement" retirees were some of the same people who asked me how I stayed so young.

About "Staying Young"

I want to emphasize that "staying young" is not possible and anyone suggesting it is possible is selling snake oil. There is no pill or product (yet) that can turn back time. However, looking young is relatively easy. With the variety of cosmetic procedures now available, and becoming more affordable, any woman can look younger than springtime as long as she takes care of herself with diet and exercise, has money, a credit card, or an Uncle Sugar.

While it is impossible to physically stay young, it is possible to hang on to some of the best gifts of youth. However, it must be understood that hanging on to those gifts takes dedicated effort. It requires regular, consistent effort, and as daunting as that might seem, look at it this way: Even if it takes 10 years to reach a desired goal, so what? You will be alive during those ten years anyway so you may as well make the effort.

Let's start with exercise. If you are in decent shape at age 40, and if you exercise consistently on a regular basis year in and year out, that effort will pay off big time when you get to 50 and beyond. You will be in great shape—the envy of peers who didn't have your persistence. Remember, however, you don't exercise to provoke envy, you do it because it makes you strong, makes you feel good, and it keeps you looking younger.

Then there is diet. It is a key element in how well we age. You can't fill your body with nutritionally useless edibles day in and day out, year after year and expect to look and feel good.

Every Woman's Major Concern

Every woman is concerned about the appearance of her face. How *do* you keep it looking years younger? Gerontologist John W. Rowe, MD, author of *Successful Aging,* maintains that 80 percent of how well we age is the result of lifestyle choices made over time, not your genes. That statement applies to the mind and body as well as the face.

I have been blessed with great skin and I work hard to keep it looking 25 years younger than my age. Over the years I have changed face care regimens many times, but one thing has remained constant: a good diet, supplements, and for decades, I have consumed a daily mega dose of calcium ascorbate, a soluble, tasteless, non-acidic form of vitamin C. The government's daily minimum requirement for vitamin C is 50-90 milligrams. This is the daily intake level considered sufficient to meet the requirements of 98% of healthy individuals. I disagree.

For the record, I routinely take 20-30 grams a day of vitamin C (1000 milligrams equals one gram). There must be something to the value of vitamin C to improve the skin because more and more cosmetics companies include vitamin C in topical formulations. While that's a great approach to skin care, I prefer to get my vitamin C benefits from the inside.

If you take time to research the benefits of vitamin C you may be surprised to see how helpful it is in treating and preventing many diseases and conditions. If you were to research benefits of vitamin C as it relates to skin appearance, you would find an article, "Vitamin C and linoleic acid may slow skin aging,"[9] which reveals, a study shows, lower intakes of vitamin C in the diet were significantly associated with the prevalence of wrinkled appearance and senile dryness. The study also found that higher intakes of fats and carbohydrates were associated with increased chances of wrinkled skin appearance and skin atrophy.

Scientific evidence also supports the superb value of high-dose vitamin C in an article, *Why High-Dose Vitamin C Kills Cancer Cells*[10]

[9] http://www.nutraingredients.com/Research/
Vitamin-C-and-linoleic-acid-may-slow-skin-aging

[10] https://www.sciencedaily.com/
releases/2017/01/170109134014.htm

If you think you would like to take vitamin C in the form of calcium ascorbate, I do not recommend taking mega doses until you are able to make a properly informed decision with the guidance of a qualified nutrition-oriented health care professional.If you ask your traditionally trained physician, who probably has had very little nutrition training in medical school, s/he will likely tell you that you are wasting your money ("you will pee it out"), you will experience diarrhea (yes, you might, at least initially), you will get kidney stones, or you will kill yourself. My thinking is that you may well "pee out" excess vitamin C, but how do you know how much you need if you smoke, have an infection, you are stressed, or have some other condition that requires or could be helped by extra vitamin C? Again, don't blindly do what I do. I'm just revealing what I believe works for me. Vitamin C is not the only supplement I take but I believe it is responsible for keeping my face wrinkle free. Again, do some homework about the value of vitamin C; you too may become a "believer" as I am.

The other thing I believe keeps my skin in remarkable condition is daily use of my Clarisonic brush. If you wear makeup every day, it does a great job of taking it all off. I normally do not wear makeup other than lipstick, but when I do, I count on my Clarisonic to take off every last bit.

I love Retin A. It must be used with care but if you can get your dermatologist or cosmetic surgeon to write a prescription for you, and instruct you about proper usage and possible side effects, it's great. Please do not buy it on the Internet or use a friend's. You don't know what you are really getting and you may end up with a badly burned face.

Always ready to try something new, recently I discovered a great alternative to prescription strength Retin A. Made by Beauty Bioscience, it contains retinol packaged in a four stage system that can result in the most amazing skin improvement I have ever seen. Because the strength of retinol is gradually increased from stage to stage, allowing the skin to become accustomed to the increasing strengths, skin irritation is minimal. My skin, as good as it is, looks completely pore less and smooth as silk since using the system. It may not work for everyone or be right for everyone, but it works for me. One of the best places to purchase it is on HSN. (I have no financial interest in the product.)

I have not found any exceptional moisturizers, including those that contain hyaluronic acid or argan oil, so I use "whatever" moisturizer from the drug store.

So there you are—my secret weapons for lasting youthfulness—at least for my looks. We can't stay young forever but we can look better than expected when we learn to use some effective tips and tools.

Staying Youthful—Absolutely Doable

While staying young is impossible, we *can* stay youthful. It is absolutely doable. This is how:

- *Managing your thinking and avoiding the traditional retired lifestyle are basic to staying youthful.* **Remember, your body eventually becomes what you think about yourself, and how you live!**

- *Stay youthful by avoiding the traditional "I am entitled" senior mindset and a cloistered, regimented, leisure-oriented lifestyle segregated by age. Both adhere to outdated cultural norms that contribute to visible signs of "old age" decline.*

- *Stay youthful by doing as much as you can to stay healthy and strong mentally and physically. Proper diet and consistent exercise starting early in life are a "must." Eighty percent of how well you age is determined by lifestyle choices made over time—not your genes, which new research indicates can be changed with a targeted diet and exercise. To learn the latest about genetic manipulation, read* **The DNA Restart** *by Sharon Moalem, MD, PhD.*

- *Stay youthful by having a purpose that benefits not just you but others. Generously share your natural and acquired gifts. Being a giver pays powerful dividends, perhaps not in kind, but in wonderful and unexpected ways.*

- **Remember, what doesn't grow quickly wilts and dies.** *Challenge your mind and body to do more, to keep it in peak operating growth-oriented condition.*

- *Stay youthful by ignoring your chronological age and living an Outlier lifestyle.*

Uh, oh. What is an "Outlier lifestyle"? Please do not be put off by the term. It does not mean being unfriendly, or living like a hermit. It may sound elitist, anti-social, discriminatory, segregationist, and even a bit paranoid— but it's not. It's not any of those things; it's a common-sense survival tactic. Let's see what it's all about.

Chapter 9

THE OUTLIER SOLUTION

> Outlier definition: *A person or thing situated away or detached from the main body or system, or a person or thing differing from all other members of a particular group or set.*

Being an Outlier for a retiree means living a lifestyle 180 degrees opposite the majority of retired peers. It means having the courage and determination to live the life you want, instead of doing what is traditional and expected "at your age." It means having the willingness to reject the decline imposed by a lifestyle that no longer makes sense. Being an Outlier makes you more aware of those with whom you associate. It allows you to find happiness within yourself and be yourself and express yourself in ways that encourage others to follow your example. When you are happy with yourself it's easier to be happy with others.

But how do you explain an Outlier lifestyle to others? It's not easy. How would you explain to others that you live on a desert island and enjoy it and expect those who have never lived on a desert island to relate to or understand your experience? All you can do is try to find the right words to convey what you know. That's what I'm trying to do here. I'm trying to tell younger women, as clearly as possible, how to stay youthful in their older years by living a culturally different, growth oriented, productive lifestyle after retirement. It is the opposite of what the prevailing culture encourages and supports.

As an Outlier you have more control over your life, assuming the effort made early on to maintain your mental and physical health has paid off. As an Outlier you know what's important and what's not. You are wise enough not to engage in nonsense that can clutter your mind and cause energy-robbing stress in your life.

What do I mean by "nonsense"? Everybody has their own version of it, but I define nonsense as being upset about things that next week you won't remember what made you upset. Nonsense is being forever upset with Aunt Mary because she forgot to call on your birthday. Nonsense is being upset with a friend who didn't invite you to a party. It's stewing over insignificant things and holding grudges. Nonsense is being intolerant of those who have a different point of view about life. Here's a real hot flash: Harboring grudges is aging. The face of a chronic grudge holder develops a "mean" look that is unattractive.

An aside: speaking of looks, I don't like facial hair on men because a beard is like a mask. It hides nuances of expression. A man looks entirely different with and without facial hair. Criminals grow a beard because they know it changes their appearance. I like to read a man's face but it's difficult when he is hiding behind what is often an obstructive beard. I can't imagine having a relationship with a man whose face I've never seen.

The "Real Housewives" TV shows are other examples of nonsense that grown women can waste their time and energy squabbling about. It's stressful and unhealthy. It's beyond cathartic to let go of meaningless stuff and be who you want to be and live the way you want to live, preferably as a tranquil in-control Outlier.

Instead of indulging in nonsense that disturbs inner peace and gets in the way of having loving relationships, I suggest cultivation of an "attitude of gratitude." Ignore what is negative and be thankful and grateful for all the good things in your life. Don't skimp on saying "please" and "thank you." It's always appropriate. It shows you respect and value others. It gives you a sense of happiness and well-being that is contagious.

When you are in a spirit of gratitude your face and eyes light up. It's a beauty secret any woman can have when she makes the choice to be grateful, thankful and positive. This is not "happy talk"—it is a real world certainty. Recently someone commented that I'm always so positive and she asked for my "secret." It's not a secret; my positivity is learned and practiced. When asked how I am, I always reply "fantastic." It doesn't matter how I feel, my response is always "I'm fantastic" and I usually add, "I know you are too!"

When you say you feel fantastic often enough, it becomes a mechanical response,

. . . automatically declaring you are fantastic initiates a sense of well being, a smile, and a glow on your face with a simultaneous release of "feel good" endorphins.

but the interesting thing is that, eventually, automatically declaring you are fantastic initiates a sense of well being, a smile, and a glow on your face with a simultaneous release of "feel good" endorphins. In other words, you are what you say you are. It's a powerful tool and doesn't cost anything to use.

An easy way to express gratitude is in the recognition of others in everyday ordinary situations. If you are ordering fast food (yes, I know you do—at least once in a while!) look at the frazzled young kid taking your order; smile, and say "please" and "thank you" and "you are doing a great job." S/he is so accustomed to hearing "hurry up with my order" that you may be rewarded with the biggest, most grateful smile full of train-tracks braces, and it will put a smile on YOUR face. You see, it is in giving that we get, not always in kind, but in ways that are more precious than what have been given. Being grateful and thankful is a huge element of an Outlier lifestyle.

Be prepared: an Outlier mindset and lifestyle will not get much, if any, encouragement from your traditional friends or from the culture. It's pretty much a given that dependence and togetherness is the standard for retirees, based on the assumption they are healthier and happier living among those their age and participating in age-appropriate activities. This is where I disagree. An "age appropriate" activity for retirees is hanging out at a senior center where bingo or shuffleboard may be the most challenging activities. I know programs at senior centers have improved in recent years but they are far from where they ought to be. Now they might have modified Zumba classes for younger retirees, and that's great exercise, or financial planning classes, but few of the offerings help retirees transition from a traditional decline-oriented mindset and lifestyle to a more positive, promising, uplifting and fulfilling way of life. Which makes sense because traditional leisure-oriented retirement is the culturally accepted way to live.

As for the benefit of living close to those your age, I have a problem with that "benefit."

While I understand the economics of living in a senior apartment complex for those on a budget, or even in an upscale retirement community, I don't think it's particularly healthy. (I've already covered the topic but it's important to revisit it.) By the way, communities dedicated to those starting at age 50 is crazy. What does a healthy 50-year-old woman have in common with most 80-year-olds? (The ideal answer would be "plenty" but, obviously, our culture is not there yet. Eighty-year-olds are still pretty much in decline as anyone age 80 has always been.) What is particularly troubling about this is that housing 50-year-olds with those much older modifies, and not in a good way, the cultural perception of "old"— particularly for women. For example, because the definition of "old" has been scaled down to age 50, it's not uncommon for a 50-ish woman to be referred to as a "grandma." Even if a woman is a grandmother, it's insensitive to suggest she is something she may not be. Not all women, especially younger women, appreciate being called "grandma."

Housing older people in an apartment complex for those "50 or better" is an insidious form of segregation, in my opinion. It is warehousing them and it's unhealthy, even disrespectful. It's akin to putting a dog in a kennel or putting a child in a playpen so he can't hurt himself and you always know where he is. One could argue it's a safety measure to house older people in their own "playpen" because seniors stick together and help each other. The reality is, activating an emergency bracelet or pendant would probably get a quicker response from paramedics or police than from senior neighbors who often are hesitant to answer a knock on the door.

When possible, it's better to live among neighbors of all ages who won't stick their nose in your business or watch behind curtained windows to see when you come and go (not that seniors do that, of course) and may be more helpful than having strictly senior neighbors.

As for socializing, I'm not a fan of herding older people into situations with other older people for the dubious benefit of meeting people, because many retirees are "Debbie Downers." I understand how unkind that sounds and I know it's generalizing, but I'm basing my remarks on personal experience. Some retirees' interests can be tedious and boring, probably because they have limited interests and contacts beyond their segregated lifestyle. Many don't have a clue what's happening in the world and don't care, except for knowing when their Social Security check will arrive. For some, the most exciting things they have to talk about are their aches and pains and how much they hate or love their doctor.

Boring people, regardless of age or circumstances, thwart your efforts to grow and change, pollute your vision, and intensify feelings of "Is this all there is?" You wonder why you feel cranky and depressed. What to do? When it comes to choosing friends, don't be afraid to separate the wheat from the chaff. That means, if you don't want to start thinking and acting like an unfulfilled retired senior, then don't join the traditional senior culture lifestyle or socialize with those who take part in it. It's not negative and elitist. It's a necessary survival tactic if you want to remain youthful.

Some would say it's being in denial for an older person to choose not to be part of or identify with the senior culture. After all, you are a senior. Who says you are a "senior"? When (or if) one becomes a "senior" is a choice. Refusal to categorize yourself as a senior is determination not to allow rusty, rigid tradition

Who says you are a "senior"? When (or if) one becomes a "senior" is a choice.

and "age awareness" to dictate how you should be and live. When you know who you are and what you want, what others say about you doesn't (or shouldn't) matter.

Now, let's get on to the meat and potatoes of the matter. Are you up to being an Outlier?

ARE YOU A CANDIDATE FOR THE OUTLIER SOLUTION?

Characteristics of Outliers include vitality, curiosity, independence, a desire to learn and grow, and healthy self-esteem. Because they live in anticipation of life and not death, they have a vision and a plan for the later years that includes overcoming chronological age awareness and outdated cultural and social norms. They have an active and balanced social life with friends as unique as they are. They dare to be different in a culture that values and encourages age-related compliance, conformity, and acceptance of decline.

When I say Outliers live in anticipation of life and not death, I mean they don't allow awareness of their age to control decisions about the future. For example, we often hear seniors say, "I'm too old to do that" or, "I shouldn't do that at my age" or "I probably won't live that long so I won't start a new business." Outliers never see themselves as too old to do what they want to do but they also are not stupid. They plan intelligently for the end of life. They just do not play God and assume they will be dead any time soon.

I realize many older women don't care about being productive in their retirement years, especially if they're not in good health. They want to enjoy a traditional retired lifestyle like most everyone else does, and that's fine. They should live how they choose to, and no one should suggest that a different lifestyle is better or more desirable for them. Live and let live.

The thing is this: We are living in a rapidly changing world with a volatile economy. Many boomers have not planned well and won't be able to afford the luxury of a typical traditional carefree retirement. Even if Social Security payments continue, if inflation hits hard and health care and energy costs continue to skyrocket, retirees may not have much more than a no-frills lifestyle. Even those who retired with a substantial nest egg may need a job or their own business if they want to have the standard of living they aspire to having. If you are not yet retired or in early retirement, and you are healthy, why not prepare now to insure not just a decent income but a second life that is fulfilling and even exciting?

Exciting? Yes, in your so-called retirement years, you can have a lifestyle that is fulfilling and even exciting. Here are examples of Matures doing just that:

Lura Zerick, 83, contributes articles to the *Put Old on Hold Journal* and other publications and recently completed her sixth book. She asks, "Who says life can't be exciting at eighty-three?" She is the perfect example of a mature rock star; perhaps not according to the cultural definition of a rock star, but how many 83-year-old women do you know who not only write, but get published?

Lura chooses friends who support her lifestyle and desire to be productive. She makes no bones about not having time for "ladies who do lunch—who meet, eat, and retreat" to their rocking chairs. She refuses to allow awareness of her age stop her from doing what she wants to do. Some of her books are listed in the Resources section.

Linda J. Brown, 77, travels around the world by herself on her Social Security income, staying in hostels. She says she is homeless by choice. Everything she needs is in two suitcases and a backpack. She writes books and blogs on her two websites:

www.heyboomers.com,

www.insecretdiffusion.com

and often contributes articles to the *Put Old on Hold Journal*. She takes photos of interesting places and sells them on websites that offer stock photos for sale. Linda is planning her third, year-long, trip around-the-world's equatorial region at age eighty.

Helen Harkness, 80+, is the founder and CEO of Career Design Associates in Garland, Texas. She helps adults redesign their career and now works with teens to help them define their goals. She is author of several books, my favorite being *Don't Stop The Career Clock*. She has been a mentor and inspiration to me and countless other older women.

Barbara E. Joe, 76, has been doing volunteer Peace Corps work in Honduras and elsewhere for many years. In response to an article written by Barbara and published in the *Put Old on Hold Journal*, she wrote to me, in part:

"Thanks, Barbara, for running my article and for this whole issue. You are really challenging the stereotypes of aging, which can do as much or more to debilitate older people than actual physical or mental changes...

People, including my kids, ask me why I go to Honduras every year now at age 76, admittedly, a dangerous country, though I do take reasonable precautions. I tell them that it's just something I do and will continue doing as long as I'm able. I feel I have something to offer and that people there need me. Why stop just because I've reached a certain birthday? The same goes for my part-time Spanish interpretation work. As long as I'm offered assignments, I'll do them. Not only do I help people (I only do schools and medical), but it's interesting and a privilege to share briefly in an intimate part of so many lives. I never know who or what to expect...

I'm glad you feel much the same way as I do and that you had the idea of starting this on-line magazine, which I know is a lot of work, but we, your faithful readers, really appreciate it."

You will have to agree, Barbara Joe is an amazing woman. (Her books are included in the Resources section.) You and I may not want to do or be able to do what Barbara does and has done, but all of us can try to do more even (especially) at "our age."

Many successful older women (and men) strut their stuff but for the most part, they don't flaunt their age or seek what I call "age publicity"—they are unknowns; they live and work "under the radar." They prefer not to talk about or reveal their age because they don't want to hear, "You are wonderful for your age." They don't want to be treated by others younger than they are with condescending "age deference." They prefer to be treated as peers. They know it is their determination and not their age that is responsible for their "wonderfulness." The reality is, productive Matures often know that once their age is out in the open, they are no longer free from annoying age-related comments and questions such as, "Why do you continue to work at your age?" suggesting they are crazy to continue to be productive.

A few words about the meaning of "age deference." If you have an ageless appearance and demeanor, meaning, it's difficult to guess your age, people tend to deal with you as their peer. They know you are an older person but until they know your exact age, they withhold expressing their personal stereotypical attitudes and beliefs about someone your age. (Trust me—everyone has *some* stereotypical

Once your age is revealed, everything changes...

beliefs about old people!) Once your age is revealed, everything changes... not with you but with those to whom your age is revealed. Their attitude toward you may flip 180 degrees, and they may not even be aware of it. It's not deliberate—subtle stereotypical notions just kick in. That's the way it is. Older people who still work understand this phenomenon and instinctively avoid making their age known. Life is easier that way.

Next, let's take a look at temperaments and personalities as they relate to Putting Old on Hold.

Chapter 11

TEMPERAMENTS, PERSONALITIES AND SUCCESSFUL AGING

Realistically, can everyone become an Outlier? Because we have free will, the answer to the question is "yes." However, it isn't always easy because certain temperaments and personalities may not allow for an easy adoption of an Outlier mindset and/or living an Outlier lifestyle.

I am always amused by seminars offered by "rags to riches" millionaires who amassed a fortune promoting personal success strategies in real estate, buying and selling fixer-uppers. Their pitch is, "Follow my advice; do what I show and tell you to do, and you, too, can become a millionaire." I would love to become rich buying and selling fixer houses but that's not me. I don't have a "wheel and deal" personality. I don't like to haggle with people (contractors, for example) who promise they will do something and don't deliver. I don't enjoy confrontation. I could be wrong, but I think the real financial winners in the "rags to riches" and other "how to" games are those who sell the "how to" seminars and books. They parlay their ability, temperament, and personality into big bucks. That said, good for them for monetizing their talents! It's too bad they don't produce more winners.

The losers are those who buy into the "how-to" game, the wanna-be hopefuls who don't have the personality and temperament or determination to get to where the hucksters say they can be. However, free will and determination can move mountains, a combination that is intensely powerful. If you want something badly enough, if you are willing to work hard enough, it's possible to succeed in spite of a contrary temperament.

Temperaments and Personalities in Retirement

Temperaments and personalities matter when it comes to dealing with aging and living in retirement. Experts say there are just four personality types: optimistic, pessimistic, trusting and envious. I believe there are others that may be subsets under those four and they are the givers, the grateful, and the dependent.

I agree there are different personalities and everyone has different goals. For example, there are "success-oriented personalities" (I can do anything I put my mind to), "failure-oriented personalities" (Nothing I do is right), "health-oriented personalities" (I will live forever), "disease-oriented personalities" (Let me tell you about my operation), "me-oriented personalities," (I deserve...) and so on. Many, even success-oriented types—the "I can do anything" people—retire simply because it's the expected and customary thing to do, or in some cases, retirement at a certain age, if not mandatory, is made clear by subtle or not so subtle company policies and actions that send the message it's time to go.

I believe those who successfully Put Old on Hold are primarily optimistic, giving and grateful. I also believe those who have the most difficulty aging well tend to have a dependent mindset because of the "you deserve" mantra that has been drilled into our consciousness starting early in the work years. Over the years we've looked forward to receiving our retirement entitlement while working at an uninspiring or tiring job. We've witnessed entitlement in action in the form of retired relatives and associates happily partaking of their owed entitlement. When we feel entitled, it's important to understand we are dependent on others to provide the entitlement. Human nature being what it is, entitled leisure is always preferred over effort that leads to decline.

While working as a pharmacist, I heard two statements from retirees over and over again: "I've worked all my life and I deserve my retirement," and "I've done for others all my life and now it's time for others to do for me." In both cases, leisure-oriented retirement was their desired prize.

If you have worked most of your adult life, then of course you are entitled to your retirement. However, but for passage of the Social Security Act in the 1930s, which designated age 65 as the appropriate age to retire, things might be dramatically different today. People might work as long as they could or wanted to. Those with foresight to prepare financially on their own might decide to stop working, or maybe not. Back in the day, families took care of each other. They lived together as often as not. If someone could not work, the family and/or neighbors did what they had to do or could do to help. A young man was not considered odd because he lived at home and contributed to the general welfare of the family. Churches and charitable institutions helped with the indigent, as they do today. The government wasn't expected to take care of anyone to the extent that it does today. Retirement communities had yet to be created. The retirement mindset and lifestyle as it exists today was just a pipe dream of social planners and visionary entrepreneurs.

It's important to note that passage of the Social Security Act resulted in more than establishment of what has become an unrealistic retirement age. As the years passed,

There is nothing wrong with believing "I've worked all my life and I've earned my retirement." It's a true statement. The question is, what will you do with your life in that earned retirement?

a well-defined leisure-oriented mindset and lifestyle gradually evolved that determined the retirement lifestyle and culture as it exists today. Del Webb and other retirement community developers certainly cashed in on the leisure-oriented retirement phenomenon. Without question, retirement has become more than a lifestyle, it has become an industry and important part of our economy.

There is nothing wrong with believing "I've worked all my life and I've earned my retirement." It's a true statement. The question is, what will you do with your life in that earned retirement? Your answer will determine how well you manage to stay healthy and how quickly you fall (or avoid falling) into decline. Much of the decline can be avoided with an Outlier mindset.

Being an Outlier doesn't mean avoiding the larger world. It just means being your own person, happily marching to your own drummer, even as your peers march together in lock step conformity and uniformity in accord with prevailing traditions and cultural norms that lead to inevitable decline.

Believing "I've worked all my life and I've earned my retirement" is powerful. It gives permission to yield to human nature that prefers leisure over effort. Here's the thing: Leisure-oriented retirement is a ticket to decline and dependence, and who wants that?

Who wants to be dependent? Remember the other statement I said I'd often hear from older people while I was working as a pharmacist? Here it is again: "I've done for others all my life and now it's time for others to do for me." It is a dependent-entitlement mindset that is begging for decline. It fails to recognize the truth in the Biblical admonition that it is more blessed to give than to receive.

I understand the angst behind "I've done for others all my life and now it's time for others to do for me." Let's say you sacrificed for someone many years of your life. You took care of an ailing parent or family member, not because you wanted to but because that's what family does and you were chosen, for whatever reason, to be the care taker. Did it make you feel used or put upon? Did you have to do without in some way? Do the memories make you feel resentful and that it's payback time?

Painful youthful memories are tough to deal with but it's crucial to let go of a mindset that can prevent you from having truly free and happy older years. Barring possible mental issues, you have a choice about what you allow to go on in your head, and you can do it without popping pills or rehashing your past with a therapist. This is not to denigrate the value of anti-depressant medication or psychological therapy, but ultimately, it comes down to a clear choice: will you continue to allow past injustices (real or imagined) to rule or ruin your life? Or will you decide the past is over and the future is a clean slate and what gets written on that slate is up to you?

Indeed, we all have different temperaments and personalities. Yes, we are entitled to our retirement, but no, we should not want the decline that is inevitable if we allow ourselves to get caught up in a dependent entitlement mindset that is a hallmark of retirement.

Take charge of your personality and temperament and make it work to your benefit, and in the process, put it to work to help others. Your determination can make it happen and you will be rewarded with a sense of freedom beyond anything you can imagine.

Chapter 12

STEREOTYPES, AGE AWARENESS, FRIENDS AND FINDING LOVE

I readily admit that trying to live an Outlier lifestyle in the retirement years requires fearless determination. Not only are you challenging the social and traditional mandate about how you are supposed to live when you retire; you must also deal with the stereotypically ignorant way older people are often portrayed or identified (by themselves or others), as well as issues with age awareness, the stigma attached to productivity in retirement, and the effect of those with whom you associate. In some way, it all affects the quality of life in the older years, especially for those trying to live an Outlier lifestyle. Let's look at some of those issues.

Stereotypes and stupidity. In spite of almost cataclysmic changes reshaping parts of the culture, archaic thinking and attitudes about aging pretty much remain stuck in the past. Mind-sets about aging and chronologically old people are tough to change because they are imposed on us starting very early in life.

Just one example is children's books that traditionally portray grandpas as feeble and/or sickly, not good for much except telling bedtime stories. Grandmas are portrayed as shapeless blobs who bake pies and babysit. At around age 50, the negativity continues with "you are over the hill" greeting cards. Those as young as age 60 are still stereotypically referred to as "old" or even "elderly—words loaded with negative imagery assigned by outdated traditions and cultural norms. Television ads for medications and insurance policies typically show older women (and men) cutting or tending to flowers in the garden, or as weak, pale and frail and in need of a care taker. Those portrayals support outdated traditional stereotypical characterizations of older women and ignore the reality that increasing numbers of older women have outgrown the old mold and feel insulted and demeaned by continuing unrealistic portrayals that marginalize and categorize them as less competent and less valuable than they are.

Listen to any nightly news report and you may hear, "A 70-year-old elderly man saved a child from..." or "The 60-year-old spunky granny shot a burglar..." We tend to see old people as senile, except when they demonstrate they are still alive and kicking, and then they are described as "cute" or "wonderful" for their age. If an older person's age must be revealed, why embellish it with adjectives that may create a negative or false image of the individual? A 70-year-old man is a 70-year-old man. Period. He doesn't need to be referred to as "elderly." A 60-year-old woman is a 60-year-old woman. If she shot a burglar, it's obvious she's spunky. Is she a grandmother? If

Is she a grandmother? If she is not, calling a woman a "spunky granny" projects an image of a decrepit old woman. It's offensive and disrespectful.

she is not, calling a woman a "spunky granny" projects an image of a decrepit old woman. It's offensive and disrespectful.

Age awareness is unhealthy concern about the number of years lived. Advanced age can cause a lot of angst for many women, especially if they feel insecure about their attractiveness. Age awareness is evident when women volunteer their age when it's not necessary. If you watch TV home shopping shows, you will notice how often an older woman, when calling in to chat with a show host selling designer jeans (or other product), proudly volunteers her age. As you listen to their conversation, you can sense when the age revelation is about to happen. The woman, whose advanced age is evident in the sound of her voice, needs assurance she is doing well for her age.

Predictably, on hearing the caller's advanced age, the show host will tell her how wonderful she is, how hip she is to stuff herself into a pair of designer jeans again, and how much younger she will look. The caller hangs up feeling elated. You might ask, "What's wrong with that?" It's pathetic. It leaves you feeling sorry that the caller feels compelled to advertise her age and buy something perhaps inappropriate in order to receive a contrived compliment from a stranger.

Another example: How often has an older woman asked you to guess her age? The woman who does that suffers so much anxiety about her age that she is compelled to regularly check to see how others perceive her, hoping for an ego-boosting response. She needs assurance that everything she does to look young is working. It doesn't matter that this tactic doesn't produce honest feedback because anyone asked to play the "guess my age" game knows the woman who asks the question needs a compliment, and as a kindness to the woman she will be told she looks younger or better than her actual age—and that's what matters.

A woman who asks others to guess her age will often volunteer her age if she thinks it will be a surprise that she is as old as she is, and she will hopefully receive a compliment. Hearing "You are *that* old? *Really*? You certainly don't look it!" is assurance she is doing very well for her age. Revealing age in this way (or in any way) is not wise because once others know your age you open yourself up to stereotypical biases, assumptions, perceptions and expectations others have about a "woman your age" and it will affect how they deal with you, and I assure you, it will not always be as you expect or would like.

Age is hugely important in our culture, especially when it comes to finding a mate. Ask any ageless woman looking for a significant other. Her attractiveness gets the attention of a man until he discovers or is told she is older than she appears. For her, a budding relationship is quickly over. The potential suitor slithers away, pouting and believing she *deceived* him and wasted his time.

As I explained earlier, there is a huge difference between others guessing your age and knowing your age. When they have to guess how old you are they are cautious—they are never quite sure how to interact with you so they tend to treat you as a peer. However, when your age is eventually revealed, their attitude and behavior toward you can change significantly. More than once I have been in a situation with younger people whose attitude and behavior changed dramatically once they learned my age.

An expectation that others may have about a "woman your age" relates to their perception of your physical and or mental competence. For example, when your age is not known, your competence is usually not in question. After your age is revealed you may find that those who formerly dealt with you as a competent peer suddenly imagine you may need help handling "old people" issues. For example, when you reach for something, you may hear, "Let me help you get that," or "Be careful, don't fall." Or, when you explain something to someone and are slow to find the right words, someone may jump in with, "What she means is...." *Everyone* is less than articulate at times, but it doesn't mean there is a loss of mental competence.

As a woman close to or in early retirement, you have a special challenge, particularly if are you the epitome of the sizzling ageless boomer babe who women envy or try to emulate.

You work hard to stay in shape, look hot in your skinny jeans and project an "I Am Woman, Hear Me Roar" image in your leather biker jacket. When you walk into a room of your peers, they glare at your hotness with obvious resentment that clearly says, "Who do YOU think YOU are?" Yeah, it's tough being a gorgeous older woman, but isn't it fun?

Because you work so hard to keep the heat turned up, you probably think the sizzle is going to last forever, but it's not. Be prepared.

I have a few hot flashes for you. Right now you may consider yourself "hot" and undoubtedly you are, but be aware that once you get to retirement age, through no fault of your own, your hotness will slowly dissipate and you will become "retirement cute" especially if you do, say, or believe something different than what's expected of you "at your age."

Once you become "retirement cute," you are good for giggles. For example, if you are single and make it known you'd like to have a guy in your life, that is soooo unbelievably cute. (Aren't the cute old gals looking for romance a riot? Those over-the-hill libidinous lizzies (wink wink) are too cute for words.)

Aren't the cute old gals looking for romance a riot? Those over-the-hill libidinous lizzies (wink wink) are too cute for words.

If by a stroke of good fortune you already have a hunky guy (giggle giggle) and he's significantly younger than you, OMG! A boy toy! That is really cute! (Let's drink to that! Aren't we thrilled for that cute old gal?)

What's super cute is if you are seen walking hand-in-hand with a lucky duck who obviously thinks you are hotter than a 10-alarm fire. That is so adorable and so doggone cute. Especially if you are wearing your skinny jeans and leather biker jacket (snicker, snicker).

Alas, there is something just as annoying as being "cute": It's being called "wonderful" for your age.

I can't count the number of times I have been told, "You are soooo wonderful for your age." I admit to being "wonderful" but my age has nothing to do with my wonderful-ness. And no, I am not "cute"; I am drop-dead gorgeous in my skinny jeans and leather biker jacket. Well, okay, maybe I'm not really drop-dead gorgeous but listen—you are what you say you are, and because I'm so wonderful for my age, I say any damn thing I want. And besides, it's so cute.

How does it happen that it's okay to demean mature women with backhanded compliments that, even though well intended, are offensive? It happens for many reasons; the most obvious being entrenched stereotypical cultural attitudes propagated and reflected, for example, in Betty White's (cancelled, thankfully) abominable *Off Their Rockers* TV show that celebrated old pranksters engaged in supposedly funny but demeaning activities to demonstrate how wonderful (and cute) they were for their age.

Regarding the *Off Their Rockers* fiasco, my friend Mary Lloyd (author of *Supercharged Retirement* and the novel *Widow Boy)* has cogently pointed out, *"No one would dream of making a series based on racist jokes or even 'dumb blonde' or other sexist jokes. Why is this ageist garbage deemed acceptable?"*

The ageist garbage is deemed acceptable because our base culture doesn't care how objectionable it is, and not only ignorantly accepts it, but celebrates and promotes it.

Unfortunately, most older women timidly recoil from confronting it. The feminist movement has done little to combat it. There is no organized rebellion and, frankly, I don't see a rebellion happening because stereotypes and entrenched outdated traditions die hard and, truth be told, old people themselves too often invite and legitimize disrespect by engaging in traditional debasing stereotypical behaviors and thinking. I'm referring specifically to demeaning "old people jokes" that old people (and not-so-old people) tell each other. Then there is acceptance by old people that it's cute to call themselves "Old Geezers," "Old Farts" or worse.

It's not cute; it's disgusting and perpetuates myths about the competence and value of old people. We've been brainwashed to accept "realities" about advanced age that are about as out of date as the horse and buggy being the preferred mode of transportation.

Every older woman in her own way deals with cultural norms that call the shots about what is and is not acceptable thinking and behavior for "old" people. My way of dealing with it is to declare I am 50 forever. Am I being "cute"? Who cares. Ignoring age-related cultural norms and outdated thinking works for me. Try it, you will like it.

The Upside of Age Awareness

Surprise! Not all age awareness is a bad thing. I'm talking about much older, inspiring Matures—Outlier types—who have lived and continue to live a growth-oriented productive lifestyle that sets them apart from the norm. They work or give performances considered possible only by young people; as a result, they are often celebrated as aren't-they-wonderful-for-their-age anomalies. In a more enlightened culture, so-called anomalies would be "unremarkable"—meaning, what they do or how they live would be considered no more remarkable or amazing than if they were young people doing the same thing. Many more chronologically older women could be truly "wonderful" for their age had they not bought into the traditional retirement mindset and retired lifestyle, and instead, continued to strut their stuff.

That said, as much as "anomalies" should be unremarkable, our ageist culture needs awareness of anomalies to help legitimize and encourage productive Matures to feel more accepted and comfortable in their Outlier mindset and lifestyle, and also, to encourage budding anomalies.

An inspiring example of a talented Mature anomaly is seen on the TV show *Britain's Got Talent*. A 79-year-old woman and her thirty-ish partner performed a dance routine that could be a challenge for 20-year-olds. As they began their routine the audience snickered and judge Simon Cowell appeared bored. By the time the pair finished their dance the audience was wild with appreciation, and even churlish Simon Cowell was awed by the performance. Watch here:

http://tinyurl.com/nrocnjz

The truth is this: Whatever you would like to do to find fulfillment in your life, your age does not determine success or failure. Chronological age is meaningless. It's simply recognition of the number of years you have lived. Your physiological age may be many years younger. You are foolish if you allow awareness of "the number" to define you or your lifestyle. What matters is mental and physical competence as well as your determination to succeed. Think about it: You are not a number. You are body, mind, and spirit, and that combination allows you to be as ageless as you permit yourself to be or will yourself to be.

When you want more out of life, but tradition says it's time to slow down, listen to your gut—it won't lie to you. Your feeling of "wanting more" is assuring you that your age doesn't matter. Your desire to be more and do more means your life force is alive and well and wants to be nurtured. So please do not dwell on your chronological age; and above all, do not allow awareness of it to negatively influence your thinking about what you are capable of accomplishing. Keep in mind that today's age 60 is the new 40; age 80 is now age 60; and that's not hyperbole, it's for real.

Recall that earlier in this book I gave the "new stages of aging" created by my friend, Dr. Helen Harkness. She is truly an ageless rock star. She has a successful career counseling business, Career Design Associates, located

So please do not dwell on your chronological age; and above all, do not allow awareness of it to negatively influence your thinking about what you are capable of accomplishing.

in Garland, Texas. In her book, *Don't Stop the Career Clock*, on page 79 she gives her new contemporary model for stages of aging:

Young adulthood: 20-40

First midlife: 40-60

Second midlife: 60-80

Young-old: 80-90

Elderly: 90 and above

Old-old: 2-3 years to live

Doesn't the Harkness model encourage you to think about where you are in life, or where you could be, and perhaps, make you realize you may have been doing yourself a disservice by seeing yourself as "old" or even "elderly" at the young age you are, and motivate you to think differently about yourself? Adopt and live by the Harkness chronology that has the potential to change your life!

Friends matter. After retirement, assuming you intend to have a growth oriented future, you will need to figure out how to meet new people who are as different as you are. Eventually friends from work will drift away and you'll be looking for new friends. Even friends outside of work will change. In your new life, new friends and associates not thoughtfully chosen can unintentionally sabotage an untraditional mindset and lifestyle, so be picky. Tradition-oriented friends are great but they can waste your time and sidetrack you if you don't have priorities in order. I recognize how business-like that sounds, but we are apt to forget that we copy thinking, behaviors and attitudes of those we associate with most often.

Women tend to be gregarious—they enjoy being with other women; their idea of social success is measured by the number of people they call "friends" as well as the number of clubs and organizations they belong to and their status on social media. This does not preclude living an Outlier lifestyle. Social connections are important and valuable for networking and even for recruiting candidates to your point of view about retirement. As I've already said—you just need to be selective and think clearly about how others fit into the lifestyle you have chosen to follow. Because we are influenced by thinking and behaviors of those we associate with most often, it's important to stay aware that associations, even on a most casual level, can make or break the quality of a lifestyle.

When looking for new friends, try to find a mentor—someone still productive who can give advice, support and direction.By the way, it's not enough to receive guidance; I suggest you mentor at least one person half your age. You have plenty of valuable life experiences and hard-earned wisdom to share. Interacting with students and younger entrepreneurs may be challenging because of generation and cultural differences, but you will get a fresh perspective on the world that will help you cope with change.

Starting retirement is a little like the transition from childhood to the teen years. When you were a teen, you didn't have the maturity to properly evaluate peers and you made many poor choices about friends. As a new retiree, until you get your bearings, you will also likely make poor judgments about potential friends, but finding appropriate friends should be a lot easier than when you were a teen because now you have life experiences to draw on and you are wiser about character and intentions of others. Again, don't choose to be friends with just anyone, and if you are single and looking for love, that also applies to finding a "significant other."

The sad reality is that women live longer, are healthier and more vital than men the same age. Many older women at 70 and beyond find themselves alone and lonely as a result of the death of a spouse. Looking for a suitable man can be difficult because eligible older men are in short supply and as often as not, they are looking for much younger women. Making the shortage of eligible men more difficult is that older men often have health issues that are serious enough to require a care taker sooner or later—mostly sooner. Undoubtedly you have heard it said that many old men are looking for "a nurse or a purse."

If you have watched Dr. Phil shows about older women desperate for love being scammed out of substantial sums of money by younger male predators they met on a dating site, it should be clear that caution and common sense are in order with dating.

The best outcome of a search for someone special would be finding a suitable younger man with a verifiable background and having the maturity and desire to have a relationship with an older woman. Since men are inclined to prefer women much younger than they are, you may think that is not likely to happen, but think positive. Not all younger men are afraid of older women. Some even prefer an older woman. If she looks good and can pass for younger, that may be all it takes, at least initially, to attract a younger man. Hit the gym (good place to meet health-conscious men) and pay a visit to your cosmetic surgeon. As I mentioned previously, there are all kinds of new surgical and non-surgical techniques and products that will take years off your appearance and give you confidence to compete with younger women who are not as savvy, wise, or sexy as you are. Whatever you do, don't settle for less than you want or deserve just to have a warm body next to you. You would be better off getting a puppy to snuggle with. Never forget that you are an extraordinary catch who deserves the best.

Now, let's take a look at the next social revolution: legalizing *perceived age*.

Chapter 13

LEGAL PERCEIVED AGE:

The Next Revolution?

Older single women often find themselves in a quandary when looking for a suitable partner simply because there are not enough available viable older men. In the previous section I suggested that looking for a younger man could be an alternative to finding someone near or at the same age as the woman. Why not?

As the saying goes, "times have changed." Indeed they have in many respects. Today, many older women appear 20-30 years younger than their chronological age. In addition, they are also physiologically younger. Have you seen 61-year-old Christy Brinkley? She looks as good now as she did at age 31 and she is not an anomaly.

It's not just that women take better care of themselves with diet and exercise, but as

I've said a couple of times, cosmetic procedures that can turn back time and are not invasive (or minimally invasive) are becoming more available and affordable. That means, if a woman is able to maintain her mental and physical health, she can look and feel ageless for a very long time.

I said it before and I feel strongly about it: I believe that a woman who looks and feels 20-30 years younger than her chronological age should not have to settle for men her age who may be "over the hill" mentally and/or physically. Men simply do not last as long as women and can require a care taker sooner than later. Yes, women can eventually need a care taker, but not as often as men. Here's a tip to help determine what you can expect from a man (from a health standpoint) as a partner as time goes on. Ask him what medications he takes. If he is taking more than two or three different drugs, that is a red flag. Do some research or ask your pharmacist what the medications are for and you will have a quick snapshot of the level of care he will possibly or probably need if you choose to have a long-term relationship with him. Why should older healthy women have to deal with that when there is a potential solution:

Legalization of perceived age identity—
the right to live the age you perceive you are.

I had been going through some old newspaper clippings and found a *Los Angeles
Times* article dated March 16, 2004, about
school trustees who complained about a law
regarding gender identity. (Which has become
a "hot" issue now.) According to the *Times* article, "The law requires schools' anti-discrim-
ination complaint procedures to reflect the
state's definition of "sex" as male or female,
and gender as a "person's actual sex or perceived sex and includes a person's perceived
identity, appearance or behavior."

The term "perceived identity" jumped
out at me. Somehow, I knew that years later
more would be happening in the name of "perceived identity" that had not been anticipated
in 2004, and indeed, more in the name of "perceived identity" has happened. As it says in
the Bible, "It came to pass."

Olympian Bruce Jenner has become Caitlyn Jenner. He said, in effect, "I perceive that
I am a woman and I will become a woman. I
want to live as I perceive myself." And it came
to pass—legally.

Thanks to the determination of Ms.
Jenner, women who would like to live their

perceived age can now hope to come out of their "perceived age closet," and live without a "number" defining their identity. But here's the problem: Caitlyn's perceived gender identity is legal, but perceived age identity is not legal, and it's not fair.

I know many older women perceive themselves to be ageless and would like to legally live their perceived age. You may be thinking, "That would open up a can of worms." Really? It can't be any more challenging than changing genders. I have thought through the most significant and practical issues involved in such a revolutionary event, and I am convinced any roadblocks could be legally and sensibly resolved. Actually, it would be so much easier than changing genders. You wouldn't have to buy a new wardrobe, learn how to apply makeup, or learn how to walk in high heels. And, best of all—no surgery is required and there would be no bathroom issues.

Legal perceived age identity is a movement waiting to happen and I think there is a good chance it could become a reality sooner than later.

Consider this: Lindsay Miller, a Lowell, Massachusetts resident and a pasta worshipping

Legal perceived age identity is a movement waiting to happen

Pastafarian, recently won a legal battle to wear the traditional Pastafarian colander head covering in her driver's license photo. The Massachusetts Registry of Motor Vehicles typically doesn't allow people to wear hats or head coverings in their license photos, but the American Humanist Association filed an appeal on Miller's behalf and won.

That achievement, as well as Ms. Jenner's transformation has set an encouraging precedent that tells me anything is legally possible.

I should have publicly declared my perceived age years ago, before an article in the local newspaper about one of my books revealed my chronological age. With that revelation things changed cataclysmically at the pharmacy where I worked. I'll give just two examples.

A male customer (much younger than I) came into the pharmacy a couple of times a week to chat. The pharmacy was busy and I had little time to socialize with customers. If I saw him coming I'd find something to do that was out of sight. Married at the time, I made certain he noticed my wedding ring but he was not deterred.

Then that fateful day the article appeared, which my admirer must have seen because...the next time he came into the pharmacy, he marched up to the prescription counter like a man on a mission, glared at me, his eyes narrowed, and he hissed, "I would NEVER have guessed you are as old as you are." To say he was angry would be an understatement. He quickly departed, never seen again. He even transferred his prescriptions to another pharmacy. If my perceived age had been legal; if I could have given my perceived age to the reporter who wrote the story, that incident would not have happened! That smitten swain would not have suffered an injured psyche, but on the other hand, I would have had to continue to deal with the nuisance and eventually he would have ended up disappointed anyway.

Next example: Before my age became public knowledge, when I worked a late night shift at the pharmacy the younger guys in the store volunteered to walk me to my car at the end of my shift. After my age exposure, that courtesy quickly disappeared. I was even avoided because, according to employee gossip, the "deceived victims" were saying "You mean she's THAT old?" They certainly didn't want to be seen in the presence of a woman THAT old! How old is THAT old? At the time I was probably in my early seventies.

I want to legally live my perceived age, which at this time is 50, and has been for the past 35 years and probably will be for the next 50 years (I'm an optimist). I want to be able to legally tell those who are nosey or curious enough to ask my age that I am whatever age I say I am, and if I choose not to provide a number, they are free to perceive I am whatever age they think I am, and I will not fear being called out as an age deceiver.

Legal perceived age is no more farfetched than Olympic athlete Bruce Jenner legally becoming a woman, or a pasta worshipper legally having a driver's license photo with a pasta strainer on her head. We are truly living at a time when anything, no matter how "far out," is possible. I am not going to wait for a legal decision; I am 50 forever.

Chapter 14

THINKING AND PLANNING AHEAD

For a rewarding retirement experience, you need a well-thought-out plan to provide balance between leisure and productivity. Whatever you plan to do, remember retirement years are your time to have the time of your life; it is the time to put the pedal to the metal and give your life as much meaning and satisfaction as you can muster!

The beautiful part of having a future-oriented plan before retirement is that it increases your chances of living on your terms and in charge of your life as long as possible. To that end there is something you really need to think about now: Your freedom. Say what? I said your *freedom*.

Not being in control of your life at any time is not fun. It is even less fun when you are older and, out of the blue, life hits you with a foul ball that is mental, physical, or financial. While you can't control uncontrollable events such as dementia, cancer or a debilitating accident, it's important to avoid "foul ball" events from happening if at all possible and planning ahead can prevent a lot of mischief.

When you are not in control of your life, especially as a result of poor or nonexistent planning, eventually, others may be in control of your life; if you are lucky, they will do their best on your behalf. If you are not so lucky, you may experience all sorts of abuse, from physical to financial. In California (and possibly your state) it's easy for someone to take control of your finances by getting a letter from a physician attesting to your incompetence. A well-thought-out and workable plan can avoid a lot of typical "who is in control of my life" issues.

Youth is free and it doesn't hang around very long, but many attributes of youth can be preserved and maintained that will go far to help insure your ongoing freedom. Think of youth as an interest-free short-term loan. If you are smart, you will hang on to the best parts of that loan and use them to your advantage. A great part of youth is a healthy, strong, flexible body that will allow you to bend and tie your shoes or pick up something, or allow you to get up by yourself when you fall. Loss of strength and flexibility puts you at a disadvantage. The weaker your body the more you may be dependent on others and a target for those who would take advantage. So try to keep physical competence as long as possible by making regular exercise and a healthy diet a priority.

Please don't gloss over the suggestion about maintaining a healthy diet and exercise regimen. It is absolutely imperative that you take responsibility and educate yourself about an appropriate exercise and diet regimen. A naturopath can provide guidance with your diet, hormone management, and general well being. Nutrition training is notoriously lacking in medical schools so a nutrition-oriented health care professional is essential because chances are you can't rely on your primary physician to know enough about prevention to help you. Whatever you decide to do to help prolong your mental and physical health—just do it on a daily basis come Hell or high water.

Conventional wisdom says it doesn't matter what you do to preserve your health; deterioration happens anyway because

Conventional wisdom says it doesn't matter what you do to preserve your health; deterioration happens anyway because decline is programmed into the genes.

decline is programmed into the genes. That's far from true. I've already mentioned that it has been established that how well you age is determined not by your genes alone but by lifestyle choices made over time. That means now is the time to get rid of a "live for today" mindset. Remember, you may have another 30 years of life after retirement and much of what happens in those years is not the result of fate but how well you plan and how well you live and have lived.

While assuming you will stay healthy as a result of good lifestyle practices, be realistic and understand that unexpected health issues may strike in later years and you need to be financially prepared to deal with them. Don't be foolish and think you are invincible.

No one is, so it's smart to have long term care insurance in place early on. If you don't think you will need it, then make certain you have a very substantial savings account that will cover very expensive care for as long as you live, which may be many more years than expected.

Whatever you plan to do to insure your freedom and autonomy in the retirement years, there will be obstacles to overcome, but obstacles test your determination to triumph over roadblocks. Armed with a can-do resolve and a plan as a roadmap at retirement, you can have and be more than what tradition prescribes.

Joyce Shafer's *Six Steps to Create a Vision for Your Life* follows. Don't read it just once; read and re-read it until it sinks in that you have to take action, and you finally understand that you don't have to be a helpless victim of a traditional decline-oriented retirement lifestyle.

Chapter 15

SIX STEPS TO CREATE A VISION FOR YOUR LIFE

By Joyce Shafer

Having no vision for your life is like being in a rowboat without oars: You go where the water takes you, or doesn't. If coming up with a vision frustrates or confuses you in any way or makes you anxious, this may help: it's not about doing but instead, it is about being, say, healthy and youthful, not just now but in the future when it's even more important. Does that shift your energy about this even a little?

Do these questions hold you back: What if I pick the wrong vision? What if by picking a vision, I limit myself? What will others think about my vision, or how might they judge it? It doesn't matter what others might

Desperation is not the energy you want flowing through you when you consider your vision.

think, because you don't have to reveal your vision to them.

Rather than think about your Vision For All Time, think about the vision of your life for the next year, or the next six months, or next month, or next week instead, to get into practice. One thing that may affect your ability to come up with a vision, whatever time-period you now want it to cover, is attempting to do this from a feeling of desperately needing to change or fix your life. Desperation is not the energy you want flowing through you when you consider your vision.

Let's get going!

Do a rough draft of your vision, so you get started on it now. Consider it an exercise only, so you ease any anxiety about doing this. Let this draft be more like play. Hand-write your draft, and write it as though it's happening now ("I wake when I want in the morning and then I...”). Let how you want to feel about your life assist you with this draft. Remember, let go of being practical, of impressing anyone or needing anyone's approval. Allow yourself the right to adjust anything in your vision that you feel the need or desire to adjust. It's like a garment you create for yourself: you must tailor it to fit you; you must love the color, texture, and feel of it. You must feel terrific when you put it on. It must feel exciting and empowering to wear it.

A vision for your life is NOT meant to be the same as a goals list and the steps to reach goals. So, try this: Write generalized specifics. What I mean is, for example, instead of coming up with a fixed amount of weight you want to lose each month, or the number of days you will exercise, state that you can do a bit better each day about food and beverage choices and moving your body. Don't impinge on your alignment with a desired target or outcome that your subconscious doesn't believe is even in the realm of possibility. Head and heart alignment is important here. This suggestion to be generalized-specific with what you write is to help you get into practice of allowing yourself to have a vision for your life each day, as well as for its entirety. When you get comfortable with this process, and with what I explain from here on, then you might want to craft a vision that is more specific, or, instead, also craft a goals list.

If it will help you, create one draft titled My Practical Vision and another titled My Magical Vision, and cut loose with this second one. What time do you want to wake in the morning, or what kind of schedule flexibility is desired? What do you want your day and what you do with it to feel like? How do you want to feel about your day and life when you go to sleep at night? How do you want to feel about your financial situation—secure or serene? And continue on, with anything you want to add. Remember: write both versions in present tense, as though each vision aspect is already happening.

Then read each vision in turn. After you read the practical version, add a paragraph about how it makes you feel when you read it and how it affects your energy; do the same after you read the magical version. Which one excites you? Which one feels like your right fit? Keep in mind that a magical vision will have practical aspects appear in your life to support it. So don't be afraid of writing down what you really want.

Once you decide on a draft vision, read your vision aloud to yourself every morning and evening for the first seven days. Each following week, spend fifteen or so minutes once a week to read your vision and feel it, believe it, trust it, and adjust it in whatever way feels right for you, because you are always changing and growing. Allow your vision to change and grow as well. Each time you make major adjustments to your vision, repeat the seven-day morning and night read-aloud process so you really get your vision into your energy field and mindset.

Release the HOW. Pay attention to inspirations that lead you to actions, then follow through on them. Never confuse activity with productivity. Inspired action is what you want to follow (not busywork), and inspiration generally comes to you when you're being quiet or still or doing something unrelated. Don't rush crafting your vision. It's important enough to take the time you need, but don't put it off either or try to write the "perfect" draft the first time. It may take a few or several tries for you to feel comfortable enough to allow yourself to write a more magical vision. And keep in mind that you want to allow the flexibility to adjust your vision as you realize more of what you really want and want to feel and allow yourself to include these in your vision.

Once your draft vision is written and it feels right, don't try to rush it or force it into your experience. Watch for signs of it taking form in your life. Watch for inspired ideas. Allow yourself to love and accept and approve of you so you allow yourself to receive your vision as your experience. It's a good practice, one you'll appreciate.

The above is taken from the article, "Do You Have a Vision for Your Life?" by Joyce Shafer, and amended slightly for our purposes, with her permission.

Joyce Shafer is a Life Empowerment Coach dedicated to helping people feel, be, and live their true inner power. She's author of *I Don't Want to be Your Guru, But I Have Something to Say* and other books/e-books, and she publishes a free weekly online newsletter that offers empowering articles and free downloads.

See what Joyce offers on her site *and* subscribe for free to get empowering articles & free gifts from her at

http://stateofappreciation.weebly.com/

Free download: *You Are More!* by Joyce Shafer: Read it, share it, download it here: *http://tinyurl.com/yzdgv9a*

Chapter 16

THE LAST WORD

At the beginning I made clear that *The New Put Old on Hold* is primarily for pre-retirees and those newly retired. I explained what I know, have seen, and experienced. I am not a 40-year-old "kid" who has done tons of research and thinks she is an expert about aging. Pushing 90, I *am* an expert!

I have chosen to address pre-retirees (boomers) and new retirees specifically because they still have time to shape the direction and content of their lives. For them, retirement does not mean the game is over. Not only can they be players, they can be game changers. They can be rock star role models of their generation and influencers of those following behind. They can show younger people that growth and productivity don't have to stop at retirement. They can help give a growth-oriented retirement a new respected status, and in the process, elevate the value and vitality of older persons.

Recall that at the beginning of the book I explained the purpose of this book, and I'll state it again here, a little more forcefully.

The purpose of this book is to encourage avoidance of the traditional leisure-oriented retirement mindset and lifestyle, because it is *that* mindset and lifestyle that accelerates premature mental and physical decline.

What you consistently think about and how you see yourself and your life is powerful because your perception of yourself, played out in your choice of lifestyle, determines what your mind and body—your life—eventually becomes. The body becomes the product of what goes on in the head.

It's just that simple. I consider the traditional retirement mindset and lifestyle a cultural cancer in serious need of a cure. I realize how harsh that sounds because so many are happy in traditional retirement, but I feel strongly about what I believe.

While I clearly support lifestyle choice in the retirement years, I don't believe that at age 65, anyone except those unable to work, should stop growing and stop being productive and instead, put their body and brains on hold to claim a politically created "entitlement" of leisure because they worked X number of years. Those eager to claim their leisure-oriented retirement prize chant, "I worked all my life and I deserve my retirement." That mantra could more accurately be stated, "I worked hard all my life and when I retire I accept my decline," because ultimately, that's the effect of traditional leisure-oriented retirement.

I know what I advocate is difficult to accept, especially if you are close to retirement, dead tired of the daily grind, unhappy with what you are doing, or just plain worn out from hard labor. I get it. But we have to start getting it that the prevailing decline-oriented retirement paradigm is resulting in far too many financially devastated, mentally and physically debilitated people. Perhaps worst of all, it's a waste of human resources and potential. Think of all the experience,

How crazy are we to allow so many priceless assets to go to waste?

education and wisdom that goes down the drain with retirement! How crazy are we to allow so many priceless assets to go to waste?

Dementia is becoming an epidemic. When coupled with "normal" retirement-induced decline it's a catastrophe. How to deal with it? Apparently, delaying retirement would be a good place to start. A study of 400,000 people has shown that delaying retirement delays dementia.[11] That needs to be taken seriously. It would help a great deal if the retirement age were raised by just one year but sadly, that's not popular. The mere suggestion results in cries of "I worked all my life and deserve my retirement." Yes, retirees must get to the Saucy Seniors Retirement Village ASAP even if it hastens decline!

For me and countless other independent women, enjoying a productive, growth-oriented lifestyle in the mature years beats the pants off the traditional retirement model. In effect, you give yourself a second life; a chance to accomplish exciting projects you dreamed of doing while tied to your work for the past forty years. Again, keep in mind that after retirement you may very well have thirty

[11] http://www.alzheimersweekly.com/2013/07/400000-people-prove-delaying-retirement.html

quality bonus years in which to live as you have never lived before. It's tragic when so many of those years are lost, thanks to a set-in-stone culturally and politically endorsed lifestyle that results in avoidable decline.

According to investigators at the University of Texas at Dallas[12], mentally challenging activities are key to a healthy aging mind.

Lead investigator Dr. Denise Park said, "...we are cautiously optimistic that age-related cognitive decline can be slowed or even partially restored if individuals are exposed to sustained, mentally challenging experiences." So the message seems to be: play golf, tennis, go hiking and biking and do what you enjoy, but remember to give your mind regular challenges that require some extraordinary effort. You will be able to function youthfully longer.

Please don't discount the importance of staying youthful and independent. As it is now, our society does not care much for old people. Younger people often see old people as a financial burden, relics who have outlived their usefulness. Respect for human life at all stages is deteriorating. Realistically, we are facing creation of review boards to determine

[12] http://www.sciencedaily.com/releases/2016/01/160115100906.htm

whether or not expensive care should be extended to old people with certain conditions. With possible health care rationing, old people are not a priority.

We live in a "throw-away" culture. Obsolescence is built into so many things so they will be thrown away in a few years and replaced. Throw-away bottles, coffee cups, soda cans and paper products add to pollution but their constant replacement keeps the economy humming.

A good example of the throw-away mentality can be seen in household appliances that depend on new technology. I have a 25-year-old Harvest Gold Maytag washer and dryer. My repairman tells me to hang on to them as long as possible because the sexy new technology-reliant appliances are expensive to fix and are designed to last but 5 years. Chances are that I will have to replace the old washer and dryer sooner than later because replacement parts are no longer manufactured—another way to perpetuate the throw-away culture.

There is concern, at least on my part, that less than perfectly healthy old people, who may be an economic burden may find themselves summarily thrown away (as a kindness to them, of course), along with millions of aborted unwanted babies. When life can be thrown away at the beginning of life it's easy to justify throwing it away at the other end. That means you need to stay strong, healthy and productive to the best of your ability.

Refuse to allow awareness of your age to dictate how you think and live. Should debilitating illness strike, (assuming your mental faculties are intact) don't allow anyone to convince you to give up your fight to stay alive and recover. With assisted suicide laws gaining favor with lawmakers, as long as you have your wits about you, don't ever allow yourself to be designated "obsolete" or not worth living and, therefore, disposable. Your life is just as precious and worthy as anyone else's, regardless of age.

However long you live, life is short. Regardless of how you choose to live it, give it all you've got. Rock it out. Strut your stuff and Put Old on Hold!

Chapter 17

R.I.P. JOAN RIVERS:
The Ultimate Outlier

Joan Rivers has passed away and I am sad she is gone. I lament her passing even though I did not care for her acerbic humor.

You had to admire her. She had guts, and if there is one thing I appreciate, it's a gutsy, successful woman who speaks her mind and goes for the gold in her life. Joan was the ultimate Outlier rock star. She avoided the traditional retirement mindset and lifestyle and her reward for doing so was an energetic, exciting, productive second life. At age 81 she was not just an entertainer but a savvy entrepreneur.

Although she was often maligned for all her cosmetic surgery, I think many older women would gladly trade their wrinkles, jowls and sagging skin for the way she looked at her age.

She was always elegantly and appropriately dressed. Her quality clothing and jewelry lines reflected her good taste. She certainly understood the power of appearance.

I don't know what Joan considered her legacy, but this I know for sure: by her example she showed older women they could live the life they want instead of blindly caving in and doing what is expected by rusty, rigid tradition.

Thanks, Joan, for your courage and chutzpah, and for being a fearless role model for all older women who want more, and are achieving more than they ever could, stuck in conventional old-fogey retirement.

RESOURCES

Read and subscribe to the *Put Old on Hold Journal*
http://www.PutOldonHoldJournal.com

Barbara Morris's Books

I Don't Wanna Be My Mother
No More Little Old Ladies
I'm Not Goin' There
The Expert's Guide to Strut Your Stuff!

Helen Harkness's Books

Don't Stop the Career Clock
Capitalizing on Career Chaos

Joyce Shafer's Books

I Don't Want to Be Your Guru
Amp Up Your Awareness
How to Have What You Really Want

Barbara E. Joe's Books

Triumph & Hope: Golden Years With The Peace Corps in Honduras

Confessions of a Secret Latina: How I Fell Out of Love with Castro & in Love with the Cuban People

Lura Zerick's Books

Getting Older and Enjoying It

River Villa

The Golden Olden Days

The House of Esther

Who Do You Think You Are?

ABOUT

BARBARA MORRIS

Barbara Morris is a pharmacist and advocate for balanced lifelong growth and productivity. She publishes the online *Put Old on Hold Journal* and has written several books on managing the aging process. In accord with her belief that it's important to continue to grow and be productive regardless of chronological age, she recently acquired her real estate license.

Barbara lives in Southern California with daughter Pat, son-in-law Bob and two rambunctious Corgis, Lola and Sam, rescued from the local shelter. To learn more, visit *www.BarbaraMorris.com*

Made in the USA
Coppell, TX
26 September 2021